The International Working Group on Women and Sport 1994-2024

This book comprehensively evaluates the role of the International Working Group on Women and Sport (IWG) – the world's largest network dedicated to advancing gender equity and equality in sport, physical education, and physical activity – in influencing global and domestic policy and practice.

The issues addressed by the IWG in its first three decades of activism reflect global socio-political progress, as well as emergent new problems, for women, sport, and human rights. The IWG's commitment to collaboration with, among others, the International Olympic Committee and the United Nations has provided the foundations for globally accepted frameworks to address gender-based issues in and through sport. The advocacy work of the IWG is told via first-hand interviews with key personnel from each of the IWG Secretariats, from its establishment in 1994 to 2024, providing insight into the most significant issues, achievements, and outcomes for the international social movement for women and sport.

The book is a useful resource for students in the sociology of sport, sport policy, leadership, management, coaching, and gender studies. It is also relevant to sport administrators, practitioners, policymakers, and those working in gender governance.

Elizabeth C.J. Pike is Professor of Sport, Health, and Exercise at the University of Hertfordshire, UK. She is also Research Lead for the International Working Group on Women and Sport 2022–2026, Project Director for the Women in Sport High Performance Pathway (WISH), co-founder of the Anita White Foundation, Fellow of the Royal Society for the encouragement of Arts, Manufactures, and Commerce (RSA), and Past President of the International Sociology of Sport Association.

Women, Sport and Physical Activity
Edited by Elizabeth C.J. Pike
University of Hertfordshire, UK

The *Women, Sport and Physical Activity* series showcases work by leading international researchers and emerging scholars that offers new perspectives on the involvement of women in sport and physical activity. The series is interdisciplinary in scope, drawing on sociology, cultural studies, history, politics, gender studies, leisure studies, psychology, exercise science and coaching studies, and consists of two main strands: thematic volumes addressing key global issues in the study of women, sport and physical activity; and sport-specific volumes, each of which offers an overview of women's participation and leadership in a particular sport.

Available in this series:

Gender Equality and the Olympic Programme
Michele K. Donnelly

The 2023 FIFA Women's World Cup
Politics, Representation, and Management
Edited by Adam Beissel, Verity Postlethwaite, Andrew Grainger and Julie E. Brice

Women in Snowboarding
Mari Kristin Sisjord

Women's Football in Africa
Chuka Onwumechili

The International Working Group on Women and Sport 1994-2024
The Challenge of Change
Elizabeth C.J. Pike

For more information about this series, please visit: www.routledge.com/Women-Sport-and-Physical-Activity/book-series/WSPA

The International Working Group on Women and Sport 1994-2024
The Challenge of Change

Elizabeth C.J. Pike

Routledge
Taylor & Francis Group
LONDON AND NEW YORK

First published 2024
by Routledge
4 Park Square, Milton Park, Abingdon, Oxon OX14 4RN

and by Routledge
605 Third Avenue, New York, NY 10158

Routledge is an imprint of the Taylor & Francis Group, an informa business

© 2024 Elizabeth C.J. Pike

The right of Elizabeth C.J. Pike to be identified as author of this work has been asserted in accordance with sections 77 and 78 of the Copyright, Designs and Patents Act 1988.

The Open Access version of this book, available at www.taylorfrancis.com, has been made available under a Creative Commons Attribution (CC-BY) 4.0 International license.

Trademark notice: Product or corporate names may be trademarks or registered trademarks, and are used only for identification and explanation without intent to infringe.

British Library Cataloguing-in-Publication Data
A catalogue record for this book is available from the British Library

ISBN: 978-1-032-41219-1 (hbk)
ISBN: 978-1-032-41220-7 (pbk)
ISBN: 978-1-003-35686-8 (ebk)

DOI: 10.4324/9781003356868

Typeset in Times New Roman
by Apex CoVantage, LLC

In keeping with the IWG's commitment to collaboration and change, this book is dedicated to two "collaborators" who changed my life for the better:

- Valerie Pike, who offered me the opportunities she never had and has been my constant support;
- Dr Anita White OBE, co-founder of the IWG, visionary, changemaker, mentor, and friend.

Contents

Preface ix
Acknowledgements x
List of Acronyms and Abbreviations xi

1 Introduction: The Challenge of Change 1

2 Reaching Out for Change, IWG Secretariat UK/Namibia, 1994–1998: Interview with Dr Anita White OBE 7

3 Investing in Change, IWG Secretariat Canada, 1998–2002: Interview with Dr Sue Neill 18

4 Participating in Change, IWG Secretariat Japan, 2002–2006: Interview with Dr Etsuko Ogasawara 24

5 Play, Think, Change, IWG Secretariat Australia, 2006–2010: Interview with Professor Dr Johanna Adriaanse 32

6 Lead the Change, Be the Change, IWG Secretariat Finland, 2010–2014: Interview with Raija Mattila and Terhi Heinilä 40

7 Determine the Future, Be Part of the Change, IWG Secretariat Botswana, 2014–2018: Interview with Dr Carole Oglesby and Game Mothibi 46

viii *Contents*

8 Change Inspires Change, IWG Secretariat
   New Zealand, 2018–2022: Interview with
   Rachel Froggatt   56

9 Share the Change, IWG Secretariat United Kingdom,
   2022–2026: Interview with Annamarie Phelps and
   Lisa O'Keefe   64

10 Conclusion   71

   Appendices
     Appendix 1: IWG Members/Global Executive   *79*
     Appendix 2: IWG Annual Meetings   *83*
   Index   *85*

Preface

This book was written to mark the 30th anniversary of the establishment of the International Working Group on Women and Sport (IWG) in 1994. The IWG's history reflects progress and continued challenges for women and sport during those three decades. This includes greater awareness of gender inequality, the benefits of participation in sport and physical activity for women and girls, as well as the benefits to society of their participation in sport. The IWG has established an international charter giving visibility to gender issues in sport, successfully advocated for legislative change, and demonstrates how social movements are most effective when combining individual activism with strategic organisational partnerships. The book is published in a year that the world's most high-profile sporting event, the Olympic Games, will be the first ever to achieve gender parity in participation and medal opportunities. The story of the first 30 years of the IWG is a story of the struggle for gender equality around the world, a story of the role of sport in societies, and a story of the power of collaboration to create societal progress and change.

Acknowledgements

This book was made possible by the generous support of the University of Hertfordshire.

Acronyms and Abbreviations

BNSC	Botswana National Sports Commission
CAAWS	Canadian Association for the Advancement of Women and Sport and Physical Activity
CBE	Commander of the Order of the British Empire
CCPR	Central Council of Physical Recreation
CGF	Commonwealth Games Federation
CONFEJES	Conférence des ministres de la jeunesse et des sports de la Francophonie
DSD	Differences in Sex Development
EOC	European Olympic Committees
ESCWGWS	European Sport Conference Working Group on Women and Sport
ENGSO	European Non-Governmental Sports Organisation
EWS	European Women and Sport
FIFA	Federation Internationale de Football Association
GIZ	Gesellschaft für Internationale Zusammenarbeit
GB	Great Britain
HPSNZ	High Performance Sport New Zealand
IAAF	International Association of Athletics Federations
IAPESGW	International Association of Physical Education and Sport for Girls and Women
ICSSPE	International Council of Sport Science and Physical Education
IOC	International Olympic Committee
IPC	International Paralympic Committee
IWG	International Working Group on Women and Sport
JWS	Japanese Association for Women Sports
MINEPS	International Conference of Ministers and Senior Officials Responsible for Physical Education and Sport
NOCs	National Olympic Committees
NZ	New Zealand
SPINS	Sport Pacific Islands Network of Sportswomen

Sport NZ	Sport New Zealand Ihi Aotearoa
TAFISA	The Association For International Sport for All
UEFA	Union of European Football Associations
UK	United Kingdom
UN	United Nations
UNDAW	United Nations Division for the Advancement of Women
UNESCO	United Nations Educational, Scientific and Cultural Organization
UNICEF	United Nations Children's Fund
USA	United States of America
WISPA	Women in Sport Aotearoa
WSI	WomenSport International

1 Introduction

The Challenge of Change

The International Working Group on Women and Sport (IWG) was established in 1994 to advance gender equality, aiming to empower women and girls in and through sport. This book is written to mark the first 30 years of the history of the IWG and its role in wider movements campaigning for women's rights as human rights. The IWG established an international charter for gender equality (the Brighton Declaration), provides advice and support mechanisms to organisations around the world, and advocates for women and sport at global forums.

The three decades in which the IWG has been operating have witnessed significant progress, as well as emergent new challenges for women and sport. The 1990s, when the IWG was established, were "an extraordinary period of great change and turmoil" (Casey, 1994, pp. 125–126). The decade had witnessed the end of the Cold War and apartheid, the development of the internet, and the rise of Third Wave Feminism, tackling issues such as a lack of women in leadership, sexual harassment, and abuse. The "change and turmoil" described by the Acting Director General of the Great Britain Sports Council in his closing remarks at the first World Conference on Women and Sport are reflected in the aims and development of the IWG. The IWG has retained a desire to advocate for "change", reflected in the theme of each of its quadrennial conferences. In seeking change, the IWG has deliberately chosen to be different in order to create positive turmoil. It disturbs the status quo in its own processes (the IWG is not an organisation but a network) and advocates for difficult and sometimes unpopular issues to advance opportunities for women and sport. As the IWG approached its 30-year anniversary, there was further change and turmoil in the world impacting women and sport, including geopolitical tensions and warfare, forced migration, climate change, the Covid-19 pandemic, and ongoing debates regarding gender identities and eligibility for sports participation. This has seen the IWG engage with what has become known as Fourth Wave Feminism, with a focus on empowerment, intersectionality, and digital communities. The history of the IWG is a history

DOI: 10.4324/9781003356868-1
This chapter has been made available under a CC-BY 4.0 license.

of women, sport, gender (in)equity, societal progress, and the power of collaboration to influence change.

The IWG was established as an outcome of the first formally recognised World Conference on Women and Sport, which was held in Brighton, United Kingdom (UK), in 1994 with the theme "The Challenge of Change". A conference like this was both possible and desirable in the context of greater awareness of the unequal opportunities that were available for women around the globe towards the end of the twentieth century and the potential of sport to empower women. The conference was part of what has been described as "a tectonic shift in the way women in sport issues were discussed and dealt with" (Pike & Matthews, 2014). This shift included giving consideration to "women on the sports agenda, and sports on the women's agenda" (Anita White, interview, 2023). In the opening welcome to the conference, Bracewell (1994, p. 3) stated, "This conference is momentous because it is the first time so many people from different backgrounds with different responsibilities and affiliations have come together to discuss women's issues in a sports context".

The IWG became one of a number of recognised groups advocating for the full and equitable participation and involvement of women in sport and physical activity. These groups include the International Association of Physical Education and Sport for Girls and Women (IAPESGW), which was formed in 1949; WomenSport International (WSI), established in 1994; and more recently, the Global Observatory for Gender Equality and Sport, established in 2021, as well as a number of national and regional groups. The existence and activities of these groups have been well documented (see de Soysa & Zipp, 2019; Hargreaves, 2000; Pike & Matthews, 2014) and have not been without their tensions, but some refer to their collective roles as a social movement or collaborative effort to mobilise action. Each of the groups advocates for women and sport by providing an evidence-base for key issues, raising awareness of them via their networks and conferences, and often successfully campaigning for legislative or policy change. The year after the establishment of the IWG, members of the Secretariat were involved in challenging discussions to ensure that the vital role of sport and physical activity was included in the United Nations Beijing Declaration and Platform for Action (1995). This has become the global blueprint for advancing women's rights, defining women's rights as a human right, and setting an agenda for the empowerment of women. Subsequent Secretariats have remained involved in the regular monitoring and updates to the Beijing Declaration, as well as informing legislative change in their own countries, as they explain in the following chapters.

The IWG is self-described as "the world's largest network dedicated to advancing gender equity and equality in sport, physical education and physical activity" (IWG, 2023). Its main activities include advocating for women and sport, monitoring progress in the international women and sport movement, and holding a quadrennial world conference. This book marks the 30th anniversary since the establishment of the IWG and responds to a claim that "the IWG, its conferences and their legacies have received scant scholarly attention" and events "that have provided opportunities for activism to transform into change have largely been ignored" (Matthews, 2020, p. 2).

The IWG is hosted by a Secretariat which is based in a different country every four years and, at the end of its term, hosts the IWG World Conference. To date, the IWG has been hosted on every continent except South America. However, the IWG has held several annual meetings in the region, supported the First South American Women's Sport Conference in 2000, and issued a statement that "It is necessary to develop an urgent South American study to support the organisation of working groups in each country" to improve the women and sport movement in South America (IWG, 1998), demonstrating its commitment to be truly global. Each Secretariat has co-Chairs and a Secretary General, all of whom were approached to be interviewed for this book. Details of each Secretariat are outlined in Table 1.1. There is also a Global Executive Board, and the full list of IWG Board Members can be found in Appendix 1.

In addition to interviewing 11 members of the IWG Secretariats (7 co-Chairs and 4 Secretary Generals), the content of this book draws on documentary analysis from the official IWG Archive. This was established during the IWG Finland Secretariat, 2010–2014, as a partnership with the Anita White Foundation (co-founded by Anita White, who organised the Brighton Conference, and Elizabeth Pike, who authored this book) in what became the Anita White Collection at the University of Chichester, UK. This archival research enabled the cross-checking of information provided during the interviews with official reports and minutes of meetings to ensure accuracy.

The book is structured chronologically with one chapter per Secretariat, and each chapter heading is the theme of the quadrennial conference (see Table 1.2). The first conference was themed "The Challenge of Change", and every subsequent conference has consistently had a theme of "change". In addition to the World Conferences, each Secretariat has also hosted annual meetings and some ad hoc events (see Appendix 2).

The following chapters will outline how the IWG is illustrative of the ways in which a global movement can be established through a combination of individual activism and organisational policies and processes, through strategic and powerful networking. This networking created the IWG network, which continues to challenge for change.

4 Introduction

Table 1.1 IWG Secretariats, 1994–2026

Secretariat	Co-Chair	Secretary General	Other key personnel
1994–1998 UK (Conference: Namibia)	Pendukeni Iivula-Ithana Anita White	Andy Hansen	Judy Kent (Conference Coordinator)
1998–2002 Canada	Pendukeni Iivula-Ithana Sue Neill	Trice Cameron (1999–2001) Deena Scoretz (2001–2002)	Kathleen Giguere (Conference Coordinator)
2002–2006 Japan	Sue Neill Etsuko Ogasawara	Yacine Kabbage	Anita White (Conference Coordinator and Senior International Advisor)
2006–2010 Australia	Johanna Adriaanse (Co-Chair, 2006–2010) Birgitta Kervinen (Co-Chair, 2006–2008; Vice Chair, 2008–2010) Carole Oglesby (Vice Chair, 2008–2010)	Carolyn Hammer-Smith Sally Ryan	
2010–2014 Finland	Johanna Adriaanse Raija Mattila	Terhi Heinilä	2010–2012 Kate Laine (Communication Manager) Essi Puistonen (Communication Manager) Niina Toroi (Communication Manager) 2013–2014 Leila Gharavi (Communication Manager) Aira Raudasoja (Conference Manager) Kaisa Larjomaa (Communication Manager) Monika Ilvestie (Assistant) Sari Kuosmanen (Trainee)

2014–2018 Botswana	Ruth Maphorisa Carole Oglesby	Game Mothibi	Boitumelo Kenosi (Marketing and Communications Manager Changu Siwawa (Resource Mobilisation Manager) Tshegofatso Matsheka (Conference Manager) Boingotlo Baebae (General Office Assistant)
2018–2022 New Zealand	Raewyn Lovett Ruth Maphorisa	Rachel Froggatt	Nicky Van Den Bos (Programme Director) Pauline Harrison (Conference Chair) Peta Forrest (Marketing & Communications Manager) Shanee Kiriau (Community & Digital Engagement Manager)
2022–2024 UK	Raewyn Lovett Annamarie Phelps	Lisa O'Keefe	Abby Burton (Strategic Communications Manager) Aoife Glass (Digital Communities Manager) Elizabeth Pike (Research Lead)

6 Introduction

Table 1.2 IWG Conferences and Themes

Year	Location	Theme	No Participants	No Countries
1994	Brighton, UK	The Challenge of Change	284	84
1998	Windhoek, Namibia	Reaching Out for Change	400	74
2002	Montreal, Canada	Investing in Change	550	97
2006	Kumamoto, Japan	Participating in Change	700	100
2010	Sydney, Australia	Women: Play, Think, Change	500	58
2014	Helsinki, Finland	Lead the Change, Be the Change	800	100
2018	Gaborone, Botswana	Determine the Future, Be Part of the Change	926	81
2022	Auckland, New Zealand	Change Inspires Change	1850 (1,200 in person)	90

Reference List

Beijing Declaration and Platform for Action. (1995). *The fourth world conference on women*. https://www.un.org/en/conferences/women/beijing1995

Bracewell, J. (1994). Official welcome. In *An international conference – Women, sport and the challenge of change – Conference proceedings* (pp. 1–2). GB Sports Council.

Casey, D. (1994). Developing international strategies. In *An international conference – Women, sport and the challenge of change – Conference proceedings* (pp. 125–129). GB Sports Council.

de Soysa, L., & Zipp, S. (2019). Gender equality, sport and the United Nation's system. A historical overview of the slow pace of progress. *Sport in Society*, *22*(11), 1783–1800. https://doi.org/10.1080/17430437.2019.1651018

Hargreaves, J. (2000). *Heroines of sport: The politics of difference and identity*. Routledge.

International Working Group on Women and Sport. (1998). *Women and sport: From Brighton to Windhoek, facing the challenge*. UK Sports Council.

International Working Group on Women and Sport. (2023). https://iwgwomenandsport.org/

Matthews, J. J. K. (2020). The Brighton conference on women and sport. *Sport in History*, *41*(1), 98–130. https//doi.org/10.1080/17460263.2020.1730943

Pike, E. C. J., & Matthews, J. J. K. (2014). A post-colonial critique of the international 'movements' for women and sexuality in sport. In J. Hargreaves & E. Anderson (Eds.), *Routledge handbook of sport, gender, and sexuality*. Routledge.

2 Reaching Out for Change, IWG Secretariat UK/Namibia, 1994–1998

Interview with Dr Anita White OBE

Introduction

The International Working Group on Women and Sport (IWG) was established as one of the outcomes of the first official World Conference on Women and Sport, held in Brighton, United Kingdom (UK), in 1994. The conference was organised by the Great Britain (GB) Sports Council, instigated by one of its directors, Dr Anita White OBE, who chaired the organising committee and subsequently became the first co-Chair of the IWG. The background to the conference, tensions between different groups before, during, and following the conference, and its immediate outcomes are well documented elsewhere (see Matthews, 2014, 2020). This chapter overviews the events at the conference, including those that led to the establishment of the IWG, and what happened over the subsequent four years, from the perspective of Anita White herself.

Co-Chair: Dr Anita White OBE

Anita White trained to be a physical education teacher, had an academic career in higher education as a researcher and teacher, then moved into sports administration as one of the most senior women in the GB Sports Council, before working as a consultant on women in sport and sports policy and sports development. She was also an international hockey player, coach, selector, and administrator. She explains that what really drove her initial interest in gender equality in sport "was a sense of the tremendous lack of fairness and lack of recognition when I was captain of the team that won the World Cup in hockey, in 1975", which extended to her appreciation for the importance of sport for all women. This led to her becoming one of the founding members of the Women's Sports Foundation in the UK in 1984; she was its Chair in the late 1980s, and this, combined with her career as an academic and in the Sports Council, enabled her to develop the international links that provided the foundations for the Brighton Conference and ultimately the establishment of the IWG.

1994: The Brighton Conference

White explained that the Brighton Conference was enabled by the support of the GB Sports Council, whose governance was primarily male-dominated, and this included their financial support for an international conference focused on women and sport. As she explains,

> we still needed to work with and through the male CEOs. It was a bit of a risk to be frank, and we really didn't know if people would come and what the outcomes would be . . . I continue to hold the view that working towards equality in sport should be the responsibility of both women and men.
>
> (White, 2018)

There was a Quadrennial Meeting in March 1994 including representatives of the Australian, Canadian, New Zealand (NZ), and UK Sports Councils, in which it was stated that women and sports meetings "should avoid being 'talkfests'" and the conference should target decision-makers rather than academics (GB Sports Council, 1994).

The Brighton Conference was originally planned to be the conclusion to the UK's term for hosting the European Sport Conference Working Group on Women and Sport (ESCWGWS). This was expanded to a more international conference given the UK's unique connections in both Europe and through the Commonwealth. As White (2018) has said elsewhere:

> We thought the time was right to try to gather people in influential positions from different countries and organisations, share experiences, identify issues, and agree a coordinated approach towards addressing them. The purpose was "to accelerate the process of change" towards gender equality in sport. And so the First World Conference "Women, Sport and the Challenge of Change" was held, organised by the GB Sports Council.

There was always the intention that the conference would bring about positive change for women and sport through the development of international strategies and networks (see Matthews, 2020), although there was no plan to have a working group before the conference took place. Records of the delegates vary, and it is usually stated that there were 280 attendees from 80 countries. However, a post-conference questionnaire from the GB Sports Council and speech delivered by Anita White confirm that the actual number was 284 delegates from 84 countries (White, 1995b).

During the conference, delegates were asked to choose a workshop in which they would explore one theme in depth over three successive 75-minute sessions. In addition, there were seminars focused on issues facing those trying to bring about change for women and sport and skills workshops offering taster sessions to help those who wish to develop leadership skills for women in their own countries. Each session was led by an expert who provided the background to the theme/issue to inform a recorded discussion of the experiences and key points discussed and agreed by attendees. The outcome of each session included recommendations for action to bring about change (White, 1995a). As White (1994, p. 2) said when opening the conference:

> The success of this conference cannot be judged so much by what happens here . . . the most important thing is what happens after the conference in different organisations and countries in different parts of the world. This is very much down to all of you represented here, to take back the ideas you have heard, and turn them into positive action for change. . . . We hope at the outset of the conference we can share a vision for sport, and that by the end of the conference we can agree international strategies to take the work forward.

This set the tone for future conferences which were targeted towards policymakers and practitioners. "That was not to ignore the role of research in informing policy and practice but the main purpose was to influence decision makers and inspire delegates to be change-makers in their own organisations/ countries" (White, 2010, p. 4). Following the conference, a report was shared which outlined examples of specific actions that different types of organisations could take to commit to the international strategy.

In terms of the international strategy, prior to the Brighton Conference, Sue Baker Finch, who was a member of the Australian Sports Commission and represented Australia on the conference planning group, proposed the creation of a charter and drafted a statement of principles drawing on national and regional women and sport policies that had already been developed in Australia, the UK, and Europe. The idea was to provide a framework that was widely acceptable to bring about change towards gender equality in sport. White explains that this draft was presented to conference delegates who were invited to send in comments, there was an open session to debate it one lunchtime, a drafting group (which included people with legal and UN experience) who listened to the comments and revised it during the conference, and it was presented to the delegates and unanimously approved on the final day.

The international strategy was addressed to governmental and non-governmental organisations, with those who committed to the strategy agreeing that they would

- endorse and commit to the application of the Brighton Declaration on Women and Sport;
- develop and execute an implementation plan reflecting full and practical fulfilment of the principles contained in the Brighton Declaration;

- nominate a representative for the purpose of communication with an international working group;
- support international cooperation by striving to send qualified representatives to future international conferences;
- provide feedback to the international working group on the effectiveness of actions taken to advance the principles (White, 1995a).

White also noted that during the conference there was a call for the work from the conference to be sustainable:

> It became clear that people wanted to see the momentum kept going, and they recognise that you needed people to do it. So, we kept getting this message from the delegates and participants at the conference, this is something really important, it needs to continue.

White discussed this with the steering group and the head of the GB Sports Council's International Affairs Department, who proposed a working group to maintain the work from the conference, with White chairing it in the first instance, along with additional Secretariat support. This had been discussed previously in a conference planning meeting, where the idea of a steering group had been proposed based on prior experience with doping control in sport, where a steering group held countries accountable for addressing doping. It was felt that this steering group (which became the IWG) could use the charter (which became the Brighton Declaration) to hold its signatories to account for addressing issues for women and sport, learning from the experience of the steering group for doping control. The immediate tasks of this group included ensuring that the Brighton Declaration was discussed at various upcoming meetings, including of the International Olympic Committee (IOC), United Nations (UN), and Commonwealth Games.

In practical terms, they then had to agree who should be on the working group to ensure that these were people with the necessary power, influence, and resources to represent their region:

> There were various regional groups having informal meetings in Brighton, so we asked each region of the world to come up with someone. And then we thought which organisations we wanted, so we wanted the IOC, we wanted WomenSport International . . . we wanted people who we thought would be movers and shakers, and be able to do something.

For the logistics, the GB Sports Council offered to provide the Secretariat with a dedicated staff member for one day a week. White undertook the role of co-Chair voluntarily, alongside Pendukeni Iivula-Ithana of Namibia, drawing on the support of the "Sports Council position, networks and office".

Relationship of IWG with Other Organisations

At the time of the establishment of the IWG in 1994, there were already other international women and sport groups. In particular, the International Association of Physical Education and Sport for Girls and Women (IAPESGW) had been formed in 1949, and WomenSport International (WSI) was in the process of being set up at the time of the Brighton Conference. There had been an International Women in Sport meeting in February 1994 which agreed on the format and outcomes of the Brighton Conference, including an intention for the Women's International Sports Coalition to formalise into WSI as an active, campaigning international lobby group which would be launched as a new membership organisation at the Brighton Conference (Sports Council, 1994). It was noted in this meeting that the launch of WSI should not conflict with or confuse the planned launch of an International Women in Sport Strategy or its Coordinating Committee (which became the IWG). White describes the reaction of WSI to the proposal to form the IWG: "I don't think they were very pleased because they thought the IWG would be competition for them. So, they were crusty and difficult relations in the early days". In subsequent years, the relationship between IWG and WSI continued to be a point of discussion as they sought ways to collaborate rather than compete, ensuring each organisation had appropriate recognition for their contribution to activities and seeking to avoid confusion for other organisations.

White explains that the IWG was very different from the WSI, with the IWG backed by government groups, with the primary strategic aim "to be a coordinating group and to try to monitor the uptake of the Brighton Declaration". At this time, the main partners in the IWG were the sports councils from the UK and several Commonwealth countries who

> met on a regular basis to discuss what they thought was important in terms of international sport development. So, for example, they collaborated on doping control, they saw that as an important issue that needed to be addressed internationally. And women, sports and gender equality is an issue in a similar vein, so they were keen to show some leadership on some of those ethical sport issues.

This also meant that the IWG was the first women and sport group which had significant material resources because it was funded by the GB Sports Council. This was indicative of a significant change towards professionalisation of the international women and sport movement and also meant that the IWG was answerable to a funder, which led to criticism, particularly from WSI, that it would not be able to challenge the male dominance of sport (Matthews, 2014).

White recognised that the groups who were initially leading the IWG work were based in the Global North, but then a Government Minister from Namibia, Pendukeni Iivula-Ithana, whom White described as having "tremendous presence", addressed the Brighton Conference inviting the delegates to Windhoek for the next meeting, and this provided the basis of the IWG's governance structure to have co-Chairs sharing the leadership of the network. In her address to the conference, Iivula-Ithana (1994, p. 29) explained how her home country of Namibia had only attained independence four years prior to the conference

> after a protracted struggle against apartheid, colonialism and foreign subjugation.... In our commitment to give to ourselves and our people the freedom and independence that many of our people have died for, the National Constitution addresses all pertinent issues of contemporal importance, among them, the position of women in our society.

Iivula-Ithana (1994, p. 30) stated that "the importance of sport cannot be over emphasised" in this commitment and clearly identified the need for global action: "Namibia is part and parcel of the international community. It is not enough when only one part of the body does not feel the pain when the rest of it is in agony".

The significance of this co-Chairing by the white European and black African woman was outlined by White:

> rather than having somebody from one of the other white Commonwealth organisations, she was coming from Namibia. ... She'd been a freedom fighter during the Civil War, and she was Minister of Sport, so she had a high level position. She'd been a politician; she was training as a lawyer. So two very different women with two very different backgrounds.

It was not possible to reach Pendukeni Iivula-Ithana for an interview, but a recorded interview with Carol Garoes, who often deputised for her in meetings, confirmed that it was important for an African country to be involved with the IWG and host a World Conference

> because it was believed then that if we host it will assist with the sensitisation and the networking to improve the status of women in sport and the girls who participate because, for years, our girls have participated in sport but they do not go beyond participation as athletes, and we wanted a situation where they can break through and reach the level of being policy-makers, coaches, managers.

(Garoes, 2013)

IWG Secretariat, 1994–1998

The IWG was deliberately set up as an informal network and not as an organisation with a constitution. White acknowledged that "there's been quite a lot of debates about (the IWG being an unconstituted network) since" but that "I think that that was probably the right thing to do". She described this network as a combination of organisational support from the Sports Council where she worked, her informal personal network of supporters, and collaboration with key organisations such as the IOC and UN, where Iivula-Ithana had excellent connections.

The aims of the IWG from 1994 to 1998 were to

- monitor the adoption of the Brighton Declaration by countries and national/international organisations world-wide;
- act as a contact and reference point, focusing on international developments on women and sport and facilitating the exchange of information;
- liaise with International Federations and multi-sport organisations;
- assist in the development and coordination of regional groupings on women and sport;
- act as a forum for these regional groupings and international women and sport organisations to review status reports and strategies and disseminate information;
- seek the inclusion of issues relating to women and sport on the agendas of major international conferences and to provide advice on the content of international conferences that address issues of women and sport (International Working Group on Women and Sport, 1998).

Following the Brighton Conference, the decision was made to hold annual meetings in different countries, starting in Canada and subsequently in Indonesia (1995), Australia (1996), and NZ (1997) (see Matthews, 2014). The focus of these meetings was "looking at what are the priorities for the Women in Sport movement, what needed to be done, who had we heard from, who signed up". Specifically, White outlines the main priorities for the Secretariat at this time "to raise awareness of the gender inequality that was so pervasive in sport, and then get important institutions and organisations to actually say this is wrong, and commit to the Brighton Declaration". White feels that it is key that the priority issues come from the conference delegates and described how many requests they received from people who had attended the Brighton Conference asking for support. The UK's Secretary General, Andy Hansen, produced reports outlining who had signed the Brighton Declaration, what they were doing, and where laws on gender equality had been passed. This provided the basis for the first quadrennial IWG Progress Report (International Working Group on Women and Sport, 1998).

During the first quadrennial of the IWG, White explains that they were trying to raise awareness to challenge the existing priorities of both "women on the sports agenda, and sports on the women's agenda". In other words, that sport had not previously been considered as an important issue in women's development, and at the same time, sport "purported to be about fair play but, in fact, it was far from fair for women". The Brighton Declaration enabled them to secure commitment from organisations, who knew that they should be supporting these agendas, to acknowledge what needed to be done and demonstrate that they were supporting it. In the first four years of the IWG's existence, 217 organisations had signed the Declaration against an IWG target of 100, including the IOC, International Paralympic Committee (IPC), and Commonwealth Games Federation (CGF). The IWG was also influential in ensuring an amendment to the UN's Beijing Declaration and Platform for Action (1995) for advancing women's rights to ensure there was reference to the role of sport and physical activity in the empowerment of women and girls, which had not been mentioned in earlier drafts. This was not without its challenges, including, for example, the IOC forming its own Working Group on Women and Sport, which raised concern regarding why the IWG did not have a seat on this and whether the IOC was trying to sideline the IWG. However, White still felt that the greatest achievements of this Secretariat were establishing the network, achieving this commitment, and a "real push to the start of the movement".

The conference at the end of this first Secretariat was held in Windhoek, Namibia, with the theme "Reaching out for Change". Unlike subsequent conferences where the Secretariat was based in the country where the conference was going to be held and organised it, for the 1998 Conference the Secretariat was based in the UK. WSI had taken on the role of developing the programme and contacting the speakers, and White explains that the GB Sports Council also supported the conference organisation sending out one of its staff members, Sallie Barker, to lead on the arrangements. The conference was opened by the Namibian president, and the majority of the attendees were African women.

At the Windhoek Conference, the IWG Progress Report "From Brighton to Windhoek" was presented, which summarises progress globally against each of the principles of the Brighton Declaration but concludes with "the concern that many organisations have not translated their endorsement of the Brighton Declaration and stated commitment into the sort of actions or change that really makes a difference" (International Working Group on Women and Sport, 1998). This was the first Progress Report, which has become one of the key outputs of IWG Secretariats every four years since 1998. As a result, the legacy of this first Secretariat was the Windhoek Call to Action, which moves from statements of principle and raising awareness to action and translating policy into practice. It was agreed that the IWG should continue in its role as the international coordinating mechanism to ensure the process of change continued.

Progress since 1998

Following the co-hosting of the Secretariat and World Conference by the UK and Namibia, an African Women in Sport Association was admitted as a full member of the Supreme Council of Sport in 1999 (Garoes, 2013). Garoes explained that this was initially viewed as a threat because, while the focus was on gender equality, men felt that they would be isolated and lose power, an issue which was raised in subsequent Secretariats. However, this

> enabled us to get to the member states of the AU (African Union) to sign the Brighton Declaration. The Brighton Declaration actually set the programme of how to empower women and the promotion of women into leadership. Most of the Ministries of Sport, Sport Commissions, and Sport Councils signed the Brighton Declaration and we moved and organised and mobilised Africa from that end.
>
> (Garoes, 2013)

When the IWG was first established, the main method of communication with the network was through the quadrennial conference. White recognises that advances in technology, and the first hybrid conference in 2022, have enabled other means of communication. Her recommended priorities for the IWG going forward are the development and nurturing of the IWG network, in particular via a better understanding of which regions of the world may be less connected with the network to ensure that individuals who are trying to make a difference are fully engaged, supported, visible, and see the IWG as their home.

White also proposed "that there needs to be more sharing", in particular by a better understanding of who the key players are. She identified the Olympic and Paralympic movements, the UN, the International Federations, and also the other international women and sport organisations, including the recently established Global Observatory for Gender Equality and Sport. White stated "with some surprise" that she felt the Brighton Declaration still had currency even though some organisations had moved on and set up their own policies. The Declaration was updated to the Brighton Plus Helsinki 2014 Declaration on Women and Sport, which White feels remains a meaningful tool to promote issues related to women and sport.

> It's a way of an organisation saying, 'we believe in this thing, and we're trying to do something about it'. My disappointment with it is, I don't think often enough it's actually led to an action plan that has then made things better. I think sometimes it's just stopped with the executive ticking a box and saying, 'Yes, we've signed that'. The signing on its own is not what it's about.

To make the Declaration, and more broadly the "sharing", more impactful, White outlined the learning from Japanese colleagues, who suggested that the signing should be more ceremonial, involving leading figures in an organisation/country. This approach could be particularly effective if combined with an agreement that there will be follow-up by the IWG to see how the organisation is progressing with its action plan and a support network to assist with these. She expressed concern with what she called some complacency in the sport movement for supporting women and sport, particularly with those who didn't appreciate the struggle that there had been and continues to be in some regions, and the need for the IWG to inspire the network "to engage in social change in a proactive and positive way".

Looking Forward

In a keynote speech at the IWG World Conference in Gaborone, Botswana, White (2018) shared what she had learned from her involvement in the women and sport movement, making the following recommendations:

- **Seize the moment**: in order to succeed, the context and timing need to be right. To make progress you need both individual commitment and organisational backing.
- **Develop a network**: it is vital that women support other women.
- **Identify your male allies** and work with them: achieving gender equality in sport should be everyone's responsibility – not just the responsibility of women.
- **Value and embrace diversity**: it is so important to recognise the limitations of your own knowledge and experience and appreciate that there are different ways of thinking and being in different cultures. For the women and sport movement to grow we need scholars and activists, people from governmental and non-governmental organisations, radical and liberal feminists and those who do not even consider themselves feminists. We have much to learn from each other.

Reference List

Beijing Declaration and Platform for Action. (1995). *The fourth world conference on women.* https://www.un.org/en/conferences/women/beijing1995.

Garoes, C. (2013, April 30). *Sports in Africa.* www.youtube.com/watch?app=desktop&v=NhdqP8emT_g. 30

GB Sports Council. (1994, March 28). *Notes of discussion: Quadrennial meeting.* Anita White Collection: University of Chichester.

Iivula-Ithana, P. (1994). Bringing about change. In *An international conference – Women, sport and the challenge of change – Conference proceedings* (pp. 29–32). London: GB Sports Council.

International Working Group on Women and Sport. (1998). *Women and sport: From Brighton to Windhoek, facing the challenge.* UK Sports Council.

Matthews, J. J. K. (2014). *A critical analysis of the development, outcomes and definition of the Women and Sport Movement (W&SM)* [Unpublished PhD thesis, University of Southampton].

Matthews, J. J. K. (2020). The Brighton conference on women and sport. *Sport in History*, *41*(1), 98–130. https//doi.org/10.1080/17460263.2020.1730943

Sports Council. (1994, February 2–4). *Report: International women in sport meetings*. Sports Council.

White, A. (1994). Official welcome. In *An international conference – Women, sport and the challenge of change – Conference proceedings* (pp. 1–2). GB Sports Council.

White, A. (1995a, Summer). Women, sport and the challenge of change: A global initiative. *ICHPER.SD Journal*, *XXXI*(4), 28–33.

White, A. (1995b, May). *The Brighton declaration: One year on*. In *World forum on physical activity and sport, Quebec*. Anita White Collection: University of Chichester.

White, A. (2018, May). *IWG leadership. In the beginning.... Keynote presentation*. In *IWG 7th world conference, Botswana, 2018*. Anita White Collection: University of Chichester.

White, A. (2010). *IWG issues past and present: Some background notes in advance of meeting August 26th*. Anita White Collection: University of Chichester.

3 Investing in Change, IWG Secretariat Canada, 1998–2002

Interview with Dr Sue Neill

Introduction

The Windhoek conference in 1998 was unusual in that the IWG Secretariat had been hosted by the UK during the quadrennial leading up to the conference, while the conference was hosted by Namibia. Following this conference, the Secretariat moved to Canada and established the pattern that has remained since then, that the World Conference is held at the end of the term of the Secretariat in the host country. The conference of the Canadian Secretariat was held in Montreal in 2002.

The co-Chair of the Canadian Secretariat was Dr Sue Neill, who used her position as a Director of Sport Policy for the Canadian government to bring the IWG Secretariat to Canada and under whose leadership the IWG transitioned from a small, primarily volunteer-led initiative to a network with the full backing of government institutions. The initial Secretary General was Trice Cameron, who was later replaced by Deena Scoretz.

Co-Chair: Dr Sue Neill

Dr Sue Neill describes herself as a "sport junkie". She studied for a Bachelor of Physical and Health Education at the University of Toronto, progressing to gain a Master of Science from the University of Alberta. Her early athletic career also included playing volleyball and field hockey at the university level, subsequently being inducted into the Halls of Fame in both Toronto and Alberta. After completing her master's, Neill stayed on at the University of Alberta as a professor in the physical education department. She also served as women's athletic director, overseeing varsity sports from 1975 to 1986, as well as coaching field hockey at the provincial and national level. This role opened Neill's eyes to the glaring inequities female athletes faced compared to the far better supported men's programmes. As she recalls:

> I was teaching there, but I was also the women's athletic director, and it was at that time where I would bump up always against, you know the men having the better schedules, the better budgets, the better coaches, the

DOI: 10.4324/9781003356868-3

This chapter has been made available under a CC-BY 4.0 license.

better everything, and it was a real struggle there. So, I guess that's where I first sort of got it – well, I first became aware shall I say that there was an issue here that needed some resolution.

Advocating for her female student-athletes fuelled Neill's passion for advancing women's sport. After finishing her PhD in educational administration at the University of Ottawa, she was given a contract with the government in the sport department, staying on as a full-time employee with the government working in sport policy, national sport policy, and international sport policy.

While working for the Government of Canada, Neill explains that "there was a priority on increasing opportunities for girls and women in sport". Her initial focus was at a national level, but she started to work with Marion Lay (co-founder of the Canadian Association for the Advancement of Women and Sport and Physical Activity (CAAWS)), who was working with the Canadian Federal Government. Neill, Lay, and Anne Hall (a Canadian researcher who specialises in gender relations in sport) started to consider how to do more work internationally. This was around the time of the Brighton Conference, which started them on their journey to be involved with the Brighton Declaration and IWG.

Relationship of IWG with Other Organisations

Neill describes how she was able to use her position in the Canadian government to host the IWG Secretariat from 1998 to 2002. As they approached the end of the Windhoek conference in 1998, no one had stepped forward to host the next Secretariat or conference. Neill describes what happened next as "more a digging process than a bidding process". She was working as the Director of National Sport Policy at the time and explains that

> I saw an opportunity and, because of my position in the Government, I was able to get a note back quickly to the people in charge there, and asking if it would be a good thing for Canada to host this. The minister was very positive . . . and almost overnight I was able to jump up and say, we have an invitation from Canada.

Neill was then supported to become the co-Chair of the IWG alongside the existing Namibian co-Chair Pendukeni Iivula-Ithana from 1998 to 2002 and subsequently remained as co-Chair for the Japanese Secretariat from 2002 to 2006. The IWG Canada Secretariat also extended letters of invitation to form an extended IWG whose members would consult on issues, receive copies of minutes, and attend General Meetings.

The support of the Canadian government, along with members of CAAWS, was crucial to the success of the IWG Secretariat during this period. Neill identifies the Director General of Sport Canada and the Minister for Sport as key government allies, explaining that the IWG Canada Secretariat "was very Government oriented" with a committee set up within CAAWS. However, a challenge to this came with a change of minister who "insisted that if the Government was going to stay involved that we would have to move the Conference (from the original plan to host it in Ottawa) to Montreal". This created a number of logistical challenges given that the organising committee and volunteers were all based in Ottawa, and most of the new organising committee operated in French rather than English. Neill was able to secure the support of Kathleen Giguere, who spoke English, French, and Spanish and was able to help coordinate the organisation of the conference. As Neill said,

> it worked out alright, but it left the little bit of a bad taste because of the work that had been done, and the people who had been involved and then, all of a sudden politics jumped in and we got moved, so that wasn't good.

IWG Secretariat, 1998–2002

During the term of the IWG Canada from 1998 to 2002, there were governmental objectives as well as women and sport objectives, with a primary focus on elevating the profile of women's sport issues across international sport governance structures, with a particular focus on women in sports coaching. As Neill reflects:

> I think, from the Government point of view we were interested in helping women in sport develop in the Americas and so we became involved in governmental organisations in the Americas. The other side of it was the Francophone side of Canada and the world, for that matter, so we became even more involved in CONFEJES, the Francophone sport body internationally.

This high-level advocacy work profoundly impacted the IWG's scope and stature, giving the Secretariat insider access to corridors of power in international government agencies that had historically been dominated by men. Neill explains that

> it's all bureaucratic stuff, but I think it was important. I always remember Margaret Talbot calling me a "femocrat", which I never responded to very pleasantly. But it probably was true in a way that I was trying to do stuff through bureaucratic channels, and I think we probably succeeded to some degree there.

The significance of working closely with governments extended beyond domestic politics. Neill was asked if she thought there was a reason that so many IWG Secretariats have been based in Commonwealth countries, and she identified that "there's a certain mentality in Commonwealth countries that are open to this kind of thing, open to opportunities, resolving inequalities".

In contrast, Neill described what she called a "combative relationship" with the International Olympic Committee (IOC) during the early years of the IWG, with IOC representatives who "would just mow right over us . . . it wasn't a good relationship at all". In particular, the IOC declined to have a representative on the IWG as they had formed their own working group, which was perceived as a potential threat that could either take the lead or sideline the IWG. Neill recognised that this relationship has improved significantly in recent years but that, at the time of the IWG Canada Secretariat, "it was hard enough for us at the international level, but it really was difficult for people on the ground who had pressures from the IOC and the IWG, and they didn't know where to go". Furthermore, in 1998, UNESCO organised an expert meeting on "Sports as a Tool for Gender Equality", which proposed the formation of an International Observatory for women and sport. Neill wrote to UNESCO, expressing her concern about "unnecessary duplication" of this proposal with the work of the IWG (Neill, 1998). It is notable that IWG representatives were invited to attend the meeting, and, in the report following the meeting, UNESCO identified that their meeting was following on from the IWG conferences in 1994 and 1998 and reinforced their collaboration with the IWG. A recommendation from the meeting was that MINEPS III (the International Conference of Ministers and Senior Officials Responsible for Physical Education and Sport) take a gender-sensitive approach to sports and physical education and give consideration to the development of an International Observatory to address the gender imbalance in sport (UNESCO, 1998). In a later IWG meeting, it was noted that members felt "the IWG should look at ways of assisting UNESCO to achieve its objectives and UNESCO representatives should be invited to conferences" (International Working Group on Women and Sport, 1998). The process to form the International Observatory was initiated at MINEPS IV in 2003, confirmed at MINEPS VI in 2017, and established as the Global Observatory for Gender Equality and Sport in 2021, supported by the Swiss Government and championed by UNESCO. The IWG and UNESCO have continued to work in partnership on issues related to gender equality and sport.

In 2002, Montreal hosted the IWG World Conference, with speakers including Billie Jean King and Dick Pound from the IOC. Neill estimates approximately 400 participants attended from across Canada and around the globe, with the conference theme focused on "Investing in Change". They had agreed to retain the word "change" in the conference title as with the previous two World Conferences in order to keep the conference results-oriented. Prior to the conference, they held a one-way workshop focused on women and sport for delegates from Pan American countries. It is notable that Neill questioned what concrete progress was made as a direct result of the conference, progress report, and legacy: "Whether I could write a list of things that were actually directly related back to the Conference in terms of enhanced opportunities for girls and women in sport, I'm not sure I could do that".

However, at the conference, the 2002 Progress Report was presented, which monitors the progress made in advancing the status of women in sport during the term of the IWG Canada Secretariat and, specifically, how well the women's sport movement responded to the 11 points recommended in the Windhoek Call for Action as an outcome of the previous IWG Secretariat. The conclusions of this report were that the best progress had been made in the areas of reaching out, leadership and capacity building, raising awareness of sexual harassment. Some good work had been done on planning and research. The report then recommended that more attention needed to be paid to physical education, the media, sharing information, government relations, and overseas development. And finally, that much more attention needed to be paid to diversity issues (International Working Group on Women and Sport, 2002a).

Progress since 2002

The legacy for the IWG Canada Secretariat was the Montreal Tool Kit (International Working Group on Women and Sport, 2002b). The Tool Kit evidences the benefits of sport and physical activity but acknowledges that special efforts are required to eliminate the gender gap and ensure sport is accessible and affordable to everyone. As such, the Tool Kit contains resources and practical guidance for different areas of change: these include advocating change, changing organisations and systems, supporting individual women and girls in sport, and preparing action plans. The Tool Kit aimed to turn the IWG's principles and declarations into implementable solutions that could drive change for gender equality in communities, organisations, and regions worldwide. However, Neill explained that "We were never able to really assess whether the Tool Kit was of use or not, you kind of hope".

Since the end of the IWG Canada's Secretariat, Neill identified two significant areas that require attention: the "huge issue" of safeguarding and the fact that the rise of professional women's sport has created new complexities around fair treatment and pay that warrant more attention:

> I think, as the lines between amateur sport and professional sport have been more and more blurred, . . . it seems to me as more and more clubs are paying athletes, as you know, more and more national teams have more and more money like from FIFA, where is that money going and are athletes benefiting from it?

Looking Forward

When asked what one change could make the biggest impact for women in sport, Neill points to the need for greater accountability. In her assessment, many organisations endorse initiatives like the Brighton Declaration but lack follow-through on implementation. She suggested that calling signatories to account for their commitments could bolster real-world change and that this needs to be more than having a policy, but there is actually some action and accountability. In Neill's view, the factor that is most limiting progress for women in sport is a failure to recognise that the world has changed and that, while it may be possible to change the culture of an organisation, this will have limited impact unless there is broader cultural change.

In addition, Neill talked about the need for investment, both in women's sport itself and by the IWG, to ensure that the conference is affordable for more people. She explained that the original focus of the IWG was on decision-makers who may be located in organisations that could fund attendance at the conference, but that this is challenging for others who do not have financial support.

On reflection, Neill highlighted the significance of the IWG being a network rather than an organisation:

> I think Canada was able to do quite a lot, and for me, personally, I got a lot, and I gave a lot, you know, so I guess it balances out. It was a tremendous experience for me that's absolutely for sure. . . .. We were kind of not a governmental, not a non-governmental body, and we could kind of float around, and bring out whichever hat seemed most opportune at the time. It's interesting experience and hopefully did some good.

Reference List

International Working Group on Women and Sport. (1998). *IWG meeting notes. Bogota, Colombia. 14–16 December 1998.* Anita White Collection: University of Chichester.

International Working Group on Women and Sport. (2002a). *From Windhoek to Montreal. women and sport progress report, 1998–2002.* www.iwginsighthub.org/iwg-leadership/resources

International Working Group on Women and Sport. (2002b). *The Montreal tool kit.* www.icsspe.org/system/files/2002%20World%20Conference%20on%20Women%20and%20Sport%20-%20Montreal%20Toolkit.pdf

Neill, S. (1998, August 7). *Personal letter to UNESCO.* Anita White Collection: University of Chichester.

UNESCO. (1998, November 28). *Summary report. Expert working group meeting on sports and gender equality.* Anita White Collection: University of Chichester.

4 Participating in Change, IWG Secretariat Japan, 2002–2006

Interview with Dr Etsuko Ogasawara

Introduction

The IWG Secretariat and World Conferences in the twentieth century were hosted on the continents of Europe, North America, and Africa in Commonwealth countries. In keeping with its cross-cultural and inclusive focus, there was an expressed enthusiasm for the next Secretariat and conference to be hosted in Asia. Dr Etsuko Ogasawara from Japan led the bid for the 2002–2006 IWG Secretariat, becoming the co-Chair alongside the former co-Chair from Canada, Sue Neill, and hosting the fourth World Conference on Women and Sport in Kumamoto.

Co-Chair: Dr Etsuko Ogasawara

Dr Etsuko Ogasawara started her career aspiring to be an international swimming coach when she was in her twenties and thirties. She was soon confronted with a reality that laid the foundations for her subsequent career to advance gender equity in sport:

> I was a swimming coach, and I really wanted to be an Olympic coach. Then male coaches told me 'you are a woman, therefore you can be a chaperone, you are not a coach because coaching is a man's job'... I was a coach, but at the national level they said that the national coach must be male.

The role of chaperone in Japan is the name given to a woman who works as a member of the coaching staff. In Ogasawara's case, she worked as the chaperone for the 1985 World University Games, the 1986 Asian Games, and the 1988 Seoul Olympics. In reality, her role was one of assistant coach, with responsibility for timings, management of logistics, and so on, which she understood was the only way a woman could become a member of coaching staff at the national level. While she accepted this, she explained that "I just thought that it was not fair, as I really wanted to be seen as a real coach".

DOI: 10.4324/9781003356868-4
This chapter has been made available under a CC-BY 4.0 license.

In the early 1990s, Ogasawara had the opportunity to travel to the United States and work for the National Institute of Fitness Sports. Here she explained:

> I saw the US coaches, and they were both men and women. The female coach was not called a chaperone, they were a coach. When I saw this . . . I wanted to study to see how we could change this situation (in Japan).

She became an intern of Women's Athletics at the University of Texas, saw that the women's athletics director had a PhD in sports management, and understood that to progress her ambitions, she also needed to study for a PhD. She studied English to meet the entry criteria and returned to the United States of America (USA) to study sports management. During her doctoral studies, she focused on women's sport as a major subject:

> I wanted to know the history, how they (the USA) were able to change that situation, because before Title IX they did not have an equal situation, but they got it. . . . That means if they could change, maybe we can change the situation in Japan too.

From studying sports management, Ogasawara learned about social ideas and creating new values through sport which could impact on society. She started to publish articles regarding women in sports for Japanese journals and realised that "the purpose is not playing women's sports at all, but also, I think that it is a chance to change Japanese society, especially the sports world, by women in sport". This laid the foundations for her involvement with, and subsequent leadership of, the IWG.

Relationship of IWG with Other Organisations

In 1998, Ogasawara had the opportunity to participate in the second World Conference on Women and Sport in Namibia, which started the process of her thinking about Japan becoming an IWG host. In order to bid for the IWG Secretariat and World Conference in 2006, Ogasawara worked with some colleagues to create a non-profit organisation, the Japanese Association for Women Sports. She explained that, in so doing, they had to consider how the acronym would work when translated into English: "JAWS, it's not good, therefore we dropped the A . . . JWS, pronounced juice, like a drinking juice, that sounds good". The challenges of a reliance on speaking English in the international women and sport movement are something that Ogasawara returns to later when the IWG Japan considered their own legacy. She explained that she approached the IWG bid in the same way she approached being a national coach: "I set out the time; in 2002 we need to announce the next conference. That means one year before in 2001 we have to bid". JWS was approved by the Japanese government, and they then spoke in public via national media to spread the idea. It is worthy of note that, in 2003, Federation Internationale de Football Association (FIFA) was hosting the Women's World Cup in China, and there was a letter from FIFA to the IWG proposing an Asian Conference on Women and Sport following the World Cup, demonstrating the reach of the IWG beyond Japan through Asia.

Ogasawara explains that the IWG Japan Secretariat benefited from her relationship with Hakuhodo, a large advertising company for whom she was an advisor, which provided JWS with access to their offices for eight years, from 1999, when Ogasawara started the process of bidding to host the IWG, to 2007, following the IWG World Conference in Kumamoto. In addition to this significant commercial partner, the Japanese Olympic Committee (JOC) was bidding to host the 2008 Olympics in Osaka. While the bid was ultimately unsuccessful, it provided Ogasawara with the opportunity to persuade the JOC that "they needed to outline their initiative in terms of gender equality or women in sports". The JOC subsequently became an IWG partner for the 2006 IWG World Conference in Kumamoto, along with JWS and the Kumamoto Prefecture Local Government.

Anita White describes the way that Ogasawara gathered support as "amazing":

> It demonstrated that things could be done in different ways – there was not one model for running IWG and organising a conference. Hakuhodo's financial support was key. The previous three conferences had all had government backing. One of the stand out aspects of this conference was the involvement of the local community in Kumamoto City which hosted the conference. They formed a citizen's group which came up with measures to improve the quality of life for local citizens, and particularly women, of all ages. The shopping arcades near the conference venue were full of advertisements for the conference and there was a wonderful reception at Kumamoto Castle. Young male and female volunteers from JWS worked hard to see that everything ran like clockwork.
>
> (White, interview for this book, 2023)

While the JOC was supportive of the IWG Japan Secretariat, during their term of hosting the IWG, relations with the International Olympic Committee (IOC) continued to be challenging. This led to Ogasawara and Neill as the IWG co-Chairs writing a joint letter to the Chair of the IOC Women and Sport Working Group, addressing questions that she had raised "concerning the IWG and its continuing relevance to the women and sport movement" and suggesting

> that the IOC and the IWG continue to relate to each other within a spirit of collaboration. . . . We would also suggest that we be publicly supportive of each other's efforts and that we demonstrate to our colleagues at other levels that we can work together towards common objectives.
>
> (Neill & Ogasawara, 2003)

IWG Secretariat, 2002–2006

When Ogasawara participated in the second World Conference on Women and Sport in Namibia, 1998, she admitted that she knew little about the international women and sport movement or conference at this stage. She learned more during the four days of the conference. On the last day, it was announced that the next IWG World Conference would be held in Canada and that it should then move to Asia, as the Secretariat and meetings had so far been in Europe, Africa, and the Americas. Ogasawara explained that, at the 1998 conference, there was only herself (who she described at that stage as being a tourist) and two people from Singapore attending the conference from Asia: "the Japanese Olympic Committee, and the Japanese Government didn't participate.... We didn't have a section or a division for women's sports, nobody was interested". This served as a catalyst for Ogasawara:

> So, I set a goal. That is, we should have a section or division to take care of this movement, not like a non-profit organisation or a small association, that would not work for Japanese society. Therefore, my goal was for the Japanese government to be interested in being involved in this movement. Then, through a sports management perspective (that she had learned from her studies in the USA), an international event would be more powerful to stimulate the Government and to show how big and how strong a women in sports global movement is . . . we should organise a conference for Women in Sports in Asia. Japan needs to lead the Asian movement for Women in Sports.

It was after attending the 1998 conference that Ogasawara also started to think about Japan being a future IWG host, explaining that "gender equality was really far from us (in Japan) at that time". The Japanese government had created a new Japanese Gender Equality Law, but "they didn't think about sports at all". For Ogasawara, being awarded the IWG Secretariat and opportunity to host a World Conference on Women and Sport was a way to "announce sport is a part of gender equality" in Japan.

She also outlined the benefits of the IWG co-Chair system:

> We really needed to explain to other people why we needed to host a world conference on women in sports, and how we should be involved in this movement . . . I needed to read, I needed a reason from the experts. This is maybe completely the opposite way of doing it, other people study and then they understand and then they start. But my case was the other way, I had an idea and then I had to study. . . . Therefore, we had different roles. So, my role was to organise a conference, and Dr Sue Neill's role was to

move the gender equality movement along the world . . . it worked well because I didn't have any background, and I did the conference.

Despite this, Ogasawara still needed to speak at numerous conferences and in English, explaining that, in the process, she accumulated knowledge and progressed from being an "actress" performing a role to where "finally in 2006 I think I got it, almost, at some level. I think so. I hope so". Ogasawara was also supported by Anita White, who explained:

> Recognising Etsuko's relative inexperience, JWS appointed me as Etsuko's international advisor and mentor. In reality, Sue, supported by the Canadian government, continued to handle the strategy and business side of the IWG including the production of the progress report, and Etsuko focussed on development of the Asian network and the 4th World Conference.
>
> (White, 2010)

The IWG Japan Secretariat produced its Progress Report in 2006 (International Working Group on Women and Sport, 2006a), which confirmed a growing recognition of the value of sport and moves towards equitable sport. The report outlines critical success factors, which include strong strategic direction, collaboration among key stakeholders, leaders championing changes to structures, policies and practice, and rigorous monitoring and evaluation processes. The Report (2006a, pp. 99–100) concludes:

> It is also clear from the most successful projects and initiatives that change, to be truly effective, must emerge from the grassroots. Only when play, sport, and physical activity become fully engrained in the social fabric of the world's communities does the desired change become possible and sustainable. Further, it is also acknowledged that sustainable change demands that women must be empowered in and of themselves and, more importantly, must take on the obligation to engrain this empowerment in the cultures and expectations of subsequent generations.

Progress since 2006

Following the IWG Japan's term of hosting the Secretariat and the World Conference in 2006, Ogasawara explained that their main achievement was the inclusion of "women in sports into the Japanese law, which means a Japanese sports policy". Prior to this, the Japan Basic Sport Plan didn't make reference to women and girls. But, following the 2006 IWG World Conference, Ogasawara was invited to speak at the National Committee Meeting:

> I had the chance to speak, 15 minutes, and our group, the JWS group, prepared a 15 minute presentation for me. It took 2 years, but they understood what kind of facts to show them. I was an actress, I presented their document, and they understood instantly.

Members of the Committee suggested that there was no need to include explicit reference to gender in Japanese law, but the learning and political support from hosting the IWG provided Ogasawara with the leverage to successfully argue that "until achieving equality, we need the word women or girls to promote women in sports".

There have been further developments in Japan since 2006. In 2011, a new sports law was introduced, which Ogasawara explains "from the beginning it says women in sports", and gender is also included in the Japanese Basic Strategic Plan. Furthermore, "every year they allocate budget to promote women and sports every year". As Ogasawara confirms, now that gender equality is embedded in Japanese law, "nobody can bother this movement".

Despite this, there remain challenges for women and sport in Japan, particularly in leadership positions: "the percentage of the board members of Japanese Sports Association is still low, and of course women as coaches remains a low number". In 2019, a new policy was created, which is the Sports Governance Code, and this sets a target for each sports association to ensure that 40 percent of the board members are women and 25 percent are from outside of the sports. Any national sports organisation which fails to meet these targets "have to explain why on the website and how they will improve".

For Ogasawara, these legislative changes are crucial because "without the document (policy), without this strong regulation, it is impossible to change something that has such a long history or long tradition". She identifies the particular importance of the support of sports ministers in government "because they have a budget, the government has such authority". In addition, she highlights the need for the support of Olympic and Paralympic organisations and Women's Rights Groups that may recognise sport as a good tool to achieve the UN Sustainable Development Goals.

Looking Forward

The outcomes of the first World Conference on Women and Sport included an international charter of principles regarding gender equality in sport, which became known as the Brighton Declaration. Ogasawara described this Declaration as "the Bible" but also outlined the challenges for those who do not have English as a first language:

> with my culture we don't use English, when you read English sentences, we didn't feel it, we didn't get it. . . . Therefore, we needed to understand the real meaning of it, that's what is most important. Not wording, wording doesn't work for the non-English speakers.

The Brighton Declaration is still viewed as important for the international women and sport movement, but the principles need to be made locally and culturally relevant.

30 *Participating in Change, IWG Secretariat Japan, 2002–2006*

As a result, the legacy of the IWG Japan Secretariat, 2002–2006, was presented as a symbol of Asian characters demonstrating an aspiration to build a network to realise gender quality in and through sport, which became known as the Kumamoto Commitment to Collaboration (International Working Group on Women and Sport, 2006b, see Figure 4.1).

熊本協働宣言

「2006世界女性スポーツ会議くまもと」参加者の賛同を得て以下宣言する。

私たちは、スポーツを通して男女共同参画社会の実現のため、世界のスポーツ界に影響を持つ関係機関および個人が密接な協働を目指すネットワークを築き、今後4年間(2006-2010)、熊本会議で生まれた積極的な「変化への参加」というビジョンを確実に推進します。

2006年5月14日

Kumamoto Commitment to Collaboration

"In order to realize gender equality in and through sport, we commit to building a network for close collaboration with relevant agencies and individuals. Over the next four years (2006-2010), we will further develop the vision of active participation in change born at the Kumamoto Conference"

Agreed by the participants in the 2006 World Conference on Women and Sport in Kumamoto, Japan. May 14, 2006.

Figure 4.1 Kumamoto Commitment to Collaboration
Source: Anita White Collection: University of Chichester

Ogasawara also offered some comments on the IWG Progress Reports: "the progress report is about the past, everything is past like an archive. Of course, history is important, however, for history we need an interpreter to read or to understand the meaning of the history". In contrast, she highlighted the importance of the IWG Insight Hub, developed by the IWG NZ Secretariat, and suggested that this should be progressed with the use of AI: "new technology will occupy us . . . we have to catch up with this. That means we need young people working with us, without working with the young people, we will die". Here she also expresses a sense that, while politicians are "changeable people", academics "are very important to lead our future students and young people".

The 2006 World Conference on Women and Sport in Kumamoto concluded with a commitment to continue the IWG for a further quadrennial. The incoming Secretariat was Australia, for which there was an open application process for the co-Chair position. Ogasawara did not continue in the co-Chair role but has remained on the Global Executive, with a demonstrable legacy for Japan since hosting the Secretariat.

Reference List

International Working Group on Women and Sport. (2006a). *From Montreal to Kumamoto – Women and sport progress report 2002–2006*. www.iwg insighthub.org/iwg-leadership/resources

International Working Group on Women and Sport. (2006b). *Kumamoto commitment to collaboration*. https://iwgwomenandsport.org/wp-content/uploads/2020/12/kumamoto_commitment_e.j.pdf

Neill, S., & Ogasawara, E. (2003, November 18). *Personal correspondence*. Anita White Collection: University of Chichester.

White, A. (2010). *IWG issues past and present: Some background notes in advance of meeting August 26th*. Anita White Collection: University of Chichester.

5 Play, Think, Change, IWG Secretariat Australia, 2006–2010

Interview with Professor Dr Johanna Adriaanse

Introduction

On the final day of the IWG World Conference in Kumamoto 2006, Sue Neill, the co-Chair, offered a concluding commitment, confirming that "the IWG has taken a decision to continue for another four years". During these four years, which marked the term of the Australian Secretariat, 2006–2010, the IWG's strategic priorities would be to have a spotlight on Oceania to offer "new opportunities" and "significant positive results in that region of the world". Further priorities were to collaborate with the United Nations and "support the Government of Greece" to ratify with UNESCO an International Observatory "for a more rigorous approach to the gathering of information and the monitoring of progress". And

> to strengthen and make more effective, strategic alliances with its traditional partners – WomenSport International and IAPESGW, ICSSPE along with the Commonwealth system, CONFEJES, the International Paralympic Committee and seek out active partnerships with key players in the global sport movement including players in the sport for development and peace movement.
>
> (Neill, 2006)

The person charged with leading this work was the IWG co-Chair, Professor Dr Johanna Adriaanse.

Co-Chair: Professor Dr Johanna Adriaanse

Adriaanse describes herself as "a sporty child" who always enjoyed playing outdoors in sailing and ice-skating and being involved in different team sports at primary school. She started to notice gender differences in opportunities for participation as she grew older when "my brothers could join soccer team, and there were not women's football teams yet". She recalled one particular occasion that had a lasting impact on her:

DOI: 10.4324/9781003356868-5
This chapter has been made available under a CC-BY 4.0 license.

I remember one time there was a new boy came in the school, and he said to me, . . . "Why, don't you go home and play with your dollies", and I said, "no, I want to play soccer". And he said "no football is not for girls. Go home".

Adriaanse didn't go home, and when the other boys selected teams, she was included, but this incident started to raise her awareness that there were gender differences in sports opportunities. Similarly, Adriaanse played hockey at the national level in the Netherlands, progressing to represent her country and win the European Cup on four occasions. During one tournament, she realised that the men's team were being accommodated in a luxury hotel while the women were in student accommodation.

Professionally, Adriaanse qualified as a physical education teacher, working in schools in the Netherlands and Italy before emigrating to Australia at age 24. She moved into the higher education sector in her late thirties, working at the University of Technology Sydney. It was here that she first became involved in the women and sport movement, when some colleagues established Women in Sport New South Wales, a state organisation for women's sport, and invited Adriaanse to join them. The organisation advocated for women's involvement in combat sports, more women in leadership positions, and increased media coverage. She eventually became the president of the organisation in 2000 and began to attend international women and sport conferences, and in 2005, she was invited to join the Board of WomenSport International (WSI), which she saw as having "a progressive agenda". Her personal experiences of different opportunities for men and women meant she realised "at those times things were not quite right for women in sport, and I think that is what drove me to become part of the women in sport movement".

Relationship of IWG with Other Organisations

Adriaanse first attended the IWG World Conference in Montreal in 2002 and described it as more passionate and practical than the traditional academic conferences she had previously attended, in what she described as "research-based advocacy". When she heard there was a call for hosts for the IWG Secretariat and World Conference, 2006–2010:

> I thought it would be nice to have it here in Australia, because when you look at it, it has been in all the other continents, Europe, Africa, the Americas, and then Asia, Japan, I thought it is probably Oceania's turn . . . and one of the objectives of the IWG is that we actually do move around the world to the different regions.

Adriaanse contacted the representative for Oceania on the IWG Executive Board who worked for the Australia Sports Commission to explore options for putting together a bid. To Adriaanse's surprise, this representative did not want to meet as she felt the conference was too expensive and she was not interested in hosting the IWG Secretariat. She described the relations with, and lack of support from, the Australian Sports Commission as "friction" and a weakness of the bid, and subsequent to Australia being awarded the Secretariat, this representative was replaced on the IWG Board with someone from the Pacific Islands to represent the wider Oceania region. The Australian Olympic Committee also declined to support the bid, stating that they did not support any activities that were only for women. "So that was a difficult situation with the Australian Sports Commission and the AOC, the Australian Olympic Committee at the very beginning, when I started to put a bid together". However, Adriaanse then received a call from the Sydney Convention and Visitor's Bureau, who were keen to host events in the area to position Sydney as a global destination. She described what happened next as "a stroke of luck". The CEO of the Bureau was an adjunct professor in her university department; he organised a meeting with the New South Wales Minister for Sport, who was also the Minister for Women, who contacted her advisories to secure funding. The Bureau put together the bid. Letters of Support were provided by the Prime Minister of Australia, the Minister for the Federal Maintenance of Sport, the State Premier, the State Minister for Sport, City Olympic Park, a number of politicians and people who wanted to bring business to Sydney, and various National Sports Organisations.

IWG Secretariat, 2006–2010

Once Australia had secured the IWG Secretariat, 2006–2010, and the World Conference 2010, the key supporters for the Secretariat were the University of Technology Sydney, who provided office space and funding for Adriaanse to attend one international meeting each year, and the New South Wales Department of Sport and Recreation, which provided funding for human resources. This included the employment of a part-time Secretary General throughout the Secretariat and a full-time Conference Manager in the final year of the Australian term. As Adriaanse said:

> It was very lean funding situation and group to do it. I did work a lot on it. But my PhD didn't progress very well during that time . . . it was challenging, even when we had the conference and all the global executive had flown in two days before, they required me still to teach the two days before they started the conference.

Adriaanse identified the additional support available to the Secretariat, which included some university interns, a representative of the Department for Women, Helen Brownlee, who was a board member of the IOC at the time, and representatives of National Sports Organisations. The meetings of the Global Executive were held in Kuala Lumpur (2007), where they were supported by a female minister for sport, Finland (2008), and Colombia (2009). She described the selection of these locations as "purposeful" to ensure that they met in different parts of the world "to make an impact in the region". In particular, the meetings in Colombia included meetings with the Colombia Olympic Committee and Department of Education in the hope that they would bid for the next IWG Secretariat. During this term, it was particularly difficult to get representatives on the Global Executive from Africa and also from Asia, other than Etsuko Ogasawara. Adriaanse reflected on the governance of the IWG, which could be time-consuming because the processes are not democratic or transparent, with some members of the Global Executive serving more terms than would be usual in organisations that have an elective process for choosing members. The Australian Secretariat trialled a process of calling for nominations and applications to be a member of the Global Executive from within the network but identified that the governance "is something that I think we haven't solved yet".

There were particular complications for the Australian Secretariat with the process for deciding who would be the co-Chairs. Adriaanse was selected as the co-Chair for Australia, and it was assumed that Etsuko Ogasawara would continue as the second co-Chair from the previous Secretariat in Japan. Initially, Ogasawara indicated she did not wish to continue, and so, during the IWG World Congress in Kumamoto in 2006, people were invited to apply for the vacant co-Chair position. This was an unusual situation, as the documented operational principles were that one co-Chair was from the country that would be hosting the next World Conference and one would be selected by IWG members (which was understood as being a member of the Global Executive as the IWG is not a membership organisation). Birgitta Kervinen from Finland was selected by a subcommittee of the Secretariat as the second co-Chair and served in this role for the first two years of the Australian Secretariat. However, she was subsequently elected as the president of the European Non-Governmental Sports Organisation (ENGSO), and, while she did not wish to resign her role with the IWG, it became clear that "she actually couldn't fulfil that role anymore and . . . she hadn't been able to contribute much because of her other appointments". During the Annual General Meeting in Finland, following a lengthy discussion "that was very difficult", it was agreed that there would be a third co-Chair, including a member of the Global Executive. This was later modified to be a Chair (Adriaanse) and two Vice Chairs (including Kervinen with Carole Oglesby, who subsequently became the co-Chair of the IWG Botswana Secretariat, 2014–2018) in order to give Adriaanse "more clout" as she was the only one generating money to run the Secretariat and host the conference. This was the governance structure from 2008 until 2010, which has reverted back to the IWG having two co-Chairs, and in the words of Adriaanse, "governance is still a bit of a problem". Anita White also identified these challenges in a report where she stated:

> A further issue is how far the powers of the Chair/Co Chairs extend in relation to the rest of the IWG. It seems that in the most recent quadrennium Johanna has made some policy decisions without reference to the group, but also that on her part she has felt unsupported by the group and so forced to take decisions independently.
>
> (White, 2010, p. 3)

The first priority for the Australian Secretariat was to put together their Strategic Plan, which was the primary focus of the 2007 Annual General Meeting (AGM) in Kuala Lumpur, where they agreed on five focus areas. Adriaanse explained that she felt it was important "to stand on the shoulders of the bid that came before us", in particular the Kumamoto Commitment to Collaboration:

> The idea behind that was that there's so many different Women in Sport organisations and groups and networks, but we needed to get them to collaborate . . . and that we also can build from each other's experience and good practices.

The other areas of focus were "to get on the agenda at the United Nations", although it was recognised at this meeting that they had received no updates on the idea for an International Observatory for more than six months. They also proposed they would "have focus on the Oceania region, and have impact, not just here in Australia and New Zealand, but also those Island nations", "the governance issue that was about that the IWG is a democratic, transparent, sustainable organisation", and host a successful conference (International Working Group on Women and Sport, 2007). During this meeting, there was also a proposal that governments who had supported previous Secretariats should be awarded special status as IWG members.

Adriaanse identified the challenges of the Secretariat relocating every four years, indicating that it took a year to finalise the Strategic Plan, and so "this stopping and starting after each 4 years after the conference we lose time, . . . and some of the momentum". Once the plan was agreed, they focused on developing a new website and a new logo. In addition, "one of the big things that we did is a regular newsletter, and we called it the Catalyst". She explained that both of her parents were scientists, and a catalyst in chemistry is a change agent, so the Australia Secretariat used the term Catalyst because "we wanted the IWG to be the change agent that collect all these elements, so to speak, different women's support groups". The Catalyst newsletter also helped address the issue that the IWG is a network rather than a legal entity, and so they were able to regularly communicate with other organisations in the network. This led to discussions with national women and sport organisations about how they could become partners, and the IWG signed a Memorandum of Understanding with 11 of them, including Canada, Colombia, Japan, Malaysia, the United Kingdom, and the United States, among others. As Adriaanse said, the other international women and sport groups, such as the International Association of Physical Education and Sport for Girls and Women (IAPESGW) and WSI, felt that the IWG should not be setting up partnerships because the IWG is a network rather than an organisation, and they felt these groups should become members of their organisation: "So that was a bit of a contentious issue".

One of the main achievements during the term of the IWG Australia Secretariat was the launch of a publication focused on women and sport at the United Nations in 2008. This was followed up with recommendations in 2009, and each year since then, during the Commission on the Status of Women, the IWG and WSI have a session on issues related to women and sport.

The end of the IWG Australia Secretariat culminated in the publication of the quadrennial Progress Report: "From Kumamoto to Sydney: Women and Sport Progress Report 2006–2010" (International Working Group on Women and Sport, 2010). This outlined key achievements of the Secretariat against their Strategic Plan, along with a number of case studies from different regions, organisations, and sports, highlighting best practices from around the globe. In particular, the report highlights the enhanced relationship between the IWG and United Nations, with joint events and a publication (United Nations, 2007) with the United Nations Division for the Advancement of Women (UNDAW) and continued plans for the International Observatory.

Progress since 2010

In November 2009, the Australian Secretariat hosted a meeting in Sydney Olympic Park of approximately 30–40 people who included athletes, coaches, sport administrators, representatives of the Department for Women, the feminist movement, and event organisers from sports venues

> and the task was to work out a legacy for the conference.... The question asked to the people was: If it could change one thing to accelerate women and sport, what should that be? And that should be, that is what we want to focus our legacy on.

The group identified issues around leadership, improved media coverage, role models, sponsorship, hosting women in sport festival, and participation. These ideas were then listed and discussed in relation to their pros and cons, with a unanimous decision that "we need to do something to get more women in leadership positions, of voices at the highest level where the decisions are made for the participants in sport". This became the Sydney Scoreboard to monitor the number of women in leadership positions, track them, and accelerate progress.

The Scoreboard was active for a few years following the Australian Secretariat, with a website and some initial data collection, which continued during the following IWG Secretariat in Finland. However, when the Secretariat moved to Botswana in 2014 and then to New Zealand (NZ) in 2018, there were not the resources to continue it, and the website and domain name were eventually closed. Adriaanse did, however, continue to track women on boards in International Federations, noting that many of them were set back during the Covid-19 pandemic in particular.

Looking Forward

Adriaanse reflected on what is currently working well in the international women and sport movement and what the priorities should be going forward. She identified the significant increases in participation in many countries, primarily in the Global North, with full stadia for major events in football, rugby, cricket, and netball, among others; the increased opportunities for women to be professional athletes with greater exposure and media coverage; and to be in leadership positions. She recognised that these opportunities were not available to women and girls in other regions of the world and that gender equality can only really be achieved if diverse stakeholders are represented in decision-making.

She identified some urgency in having male allies: "if you see it's about gender, so it's not about the difference between men and women, it's about relationships between men, women, and among the groups, and also non-binary people". She broadened this out to the importance of intersectionality in order to accelerate gender equality, recognising her own privilege as a white Western woman,

> we have access to sport, and we have access to being in leadership positions. But of course, if you are a black woman, or someone from a remote country, or from a disadvantaged community, or someone with disabilities or from the queer community, there are huge challenges.

Adriaanse returned to the focus of the Australian Secretariat on leadership, suggesting that what is needed is "not only a seat at the table, but having a voice there".

In order to achieve this, Adriaanse identified "connections" as both a main achievement of the IWG Australia Secretariat and a key focus area going forward. Key partners and supporters would be the United Nations, UN Women, the International Olympic and Paralympic Committees, and WSI, and she also suggested that more attention could be given to the ways in which the IWG can support and connect community groups.

Adriaanse proposed that the process and expectations for signing the Brighton Declaration could usefully be reviewed – moving beyond just signing the principles to ensuring that the signatories have a plan for what they will do for gender equality with targets that they have to report against annually. She provided the example of the Australian Male Champions of Change, which involved key figures in the largest corporates in Australia committing to be champions of change in their workplace. All of the champions were male, and the changes they made could be varied, including remuneration, employment opportunities, and women in leadership positions, and each year they had to provide a plan and report what had been achieved in order to retain the title of Champion of Change. This has now expanded to champions in sport, government, and different business sectors and includes women, so it is no longer the Male Champions of Change but the Champions of Change Coalition (https://championsofchangecoalition.org/), and the model is being considered by other countries.

Going forward, Adriaanse suggested that priority areas are ensuring different perspectives are heard, including giving consideration to intersectionality and the fluidity of gender, clear governance and communications between international women and sport groups. She identifies the IWG as having a vital role in ensuring coordinated, collective action through its network to keep gender equality in sport high on the global agenda.

At the end of the Australian term, the IWG Secretariat moved to be hosted by Finland from 2010 to 2014, with the Helsinki conference in 2014 marking 20 years since the establishment of the IWG.

Reference List

Champions of Change Coalition. https://championsofchangecoalition.org/
International Working Group on Women and Sport. (2007). *International working group on women and sport, 2007–2012*. [Unpublished paper]. Anita White Collection: University of Chichester.
International Working Group on Women and Sport. (2010). *From Kumamoto to Sydney: Women and sport progress report 2006–2010*. www.iwginsighthub.org/iwg-leadership/resources
Neill, S. (2006). *IWG future*. [Unpublished paper]. Anita White Collection: University of Chichester.
United Nations. (2007). Women, gender equality and sport. In *Women 2000 and beyond*. United Nations.
White, A. (2010). *IWG issues past and present: Some background notes in advance of meeting August 26th*. Anita White Collection: University of Chichester.

6 Lead the Change, Be the Change, IWG Secretariat Finland, 2010–2014

Interview with Raija Mattila and Terhi Heinilä

Introduction

The IWG Secretariat from 2010 to 2014 culminated in a celebration of 20 years since the Brighton Conference and the establishment of the IWG. The co-Chairs were Raija Iiasalo-Mattila from Finland and Johanna Adriaanse, continuing from the previous IWG Secretariat in Australia, with Terhi Heinilä serving as Secretary General. Their term witnessed complex dynamics with other organisations and regional groups, with enhanced cooperation and connections becoming a key focus of their work, not least in increasing the numbers of signatories to the Brighton Declaration. They commissioned a report to mark 20 years of progress in the international women and sport movement and used this work to inform their legacy of an updated international charter, which became known as the Brighton Plus Helsinki 2014 Declaration.

Co-Chair and Secretary General: Raija Mattila and Terhi Heinilä

Mattila and Heinilä shared similar backgrounds as women who had not competed in sport at a high-performance level but were both active in physical activity and sport, progressing to have careers in sports administration. They both initially worked for the Finnish Society for Sports Sciences, where they were responsible for communication and international affairs. Mattila moved to the Ministry of Education, where she worked for 20 years in international affairs in the field of sport, eventually becoming the Director of Sport in the Ministry of Education. In addition to her national work, among other duties, she served as the Chair of the Committee for the Development of Sport in the Council of Europe. Heinilä also worked in international relations for the National Sports Confederation.

Their work exposed both of them to the male dominance of sport, and, together with other activists, they founded a network "Women on the Move" in Finland. They identified the IWG World Conference 1994 in Brighton as "the big thing" (Mattila), "really special" (Heinilä). Heinilä attended the conference with other Finnish colleagues. The conference "gave energy to us, and

DOI: 10.4324/9781003356868-6
This chapter has been made available under a CC-BY 4.0 license.

we started systematically to work on gender issues" (Mattila). Both of them remained involved with the IWG since 1994, leading the Secretariat during the 2010–2014 quadrennial. Following the Brighton Conference, a nationally important working group on gender equality in sport (Spikes) was formed, initiated by active women in sport and established by the Minister of Sports.

Relationship of IWG with Other Organisations

Mattila and Heinilä identified the importance of their involvement in multinational organisations – initially in the European Women and Sport (EWS) and European Non-Governmental Sports Organisation (ENGSO), as well as Mattila's work in the Council of Europe and UNESCO. They explained how important it was to people in Finland, as a relatively small country, to have international networks to share their work and learn from others. These international connections were key to the decision to bid to host the IWG Secretariat: "we had experience on the European level, leading European Women in Sport. And we had participated in IWG with a delegation actively participating in the conferences, and also Birgitta Kervinen being co-chair/Vice-Chair during the Australia term" (Mattila).

The bid was not straightforward, as they faced "opposition" (Heinilä) by the Finnish Sport Confederation. However, there was strong support from, among others, the President of Finland Tarja Halonen, who became the first woman to be elected to this position in 2000, and Speaker of Parliament Sauli Niinistö, as well as a large number of international sports organisations. In particular, there was crucial financial support from the Minister for Sport. Finland won the bid, competing against six other contenders, with the awarding committee eventually choosing between Dubai (which they felt was high risk) and Finland (which they felt was secure), and Finland became the IWG Secretariat, 2010–2014.

A very early act of the IWG Finland Secretariat was to form a partnership with the Anita White Foundation, who established the IWG Archive as part of what became the Anita White Collection at the University of Chichester, UK, which provided many of the documents informing this book.

IWG Secretariat, 2010–2014

The main priorities for the Finland Secretariat built from this aspiration to create better connections with other regions of the world:

> The first two years we supported everyone who did something for gender equality and women's sport who we knew. We supported them, and brought them up in our newsletters and social media. In the end they were active collaborators with the IWG.
>
> (Heinilä)

Their work was primarily supported by the Ministry of Education, and they also drew on national Finnish representatives who served on the boards of International Federations to help reach out globally through those sports organisations. They attended many conferences where they spoke to people who told them "that IWG has changed their life" (Heinilä), largely because the IWG offered a point of contact to people: "It seemed almost like they never thought it would be possible for a woman to speak like this, or to support . . . there were many who we met during those four years" (Heinilä). There was a particular focus on the African region, primarily through the African representative on the IWG Group, Matilda Mwaba, and other regions outside of Europe.

Early in their Secretariat, a meeting was held in London, UK, to have "Informal Discussions on the Legacy of the Brighton Declaration" with UK colleagues who had been involved in the organisation of the 1994 Brighton Conference, including Anita White. In a paper prepared by White (2010), she explained that the IWG was originally set up to work

> in an informal way and initially resisted formalising our structure. We did not want to follow the male model of sports governance and believed that women could do it differently – and better! As the IWG and its conferences grew in status and recognition, people started asking how members were appointed, and there was a feeling it was a bit of an "old girls club" so in response we made the appointment process more transparent as well as publicising our structure, aims and objectives. Hence the current pattern of reps from WSI and IAPESGW, each region and coopted individuals. In 2006 we advertised the position of Co Chair to lead the group together with the Co Chair appointed by the next Conference, and Birgitta was appointed from a strong field.

They faced a number of challenges during the term of their Secretariat. They mentioned that, in the beginning of the Finnish leadership, the relationship between the IWG and the IOC "was challenging". After the first year and several meetings between Mattila and IOC Member Peter Tallberg, cooperation between the IOC and IWG "was activated and functioned in a good spirit" (Mattila). During the Finnish leadership, Mattila and Heinilä worked intensively to strengthen connections with international sports federations such as the International Association of Athletics Federations (IAAF/WA), FIFA, Union of European Football Associations (UEFA), International Boxing Association, International Icehockey Federation, and other sports federations, governmental and nongovernmental organisations. As an example of sport policy actions, they wrote to FIFA regarding women wearing headscarves while taking part in competitions. As a key decision-making activity, the Finnish leadership organised IWG Annual Meetings hosted by various bodies in Paris, Tokyo, Doha, and Vierumäki, which enabled local women to organise an international event where the Qatar Olympic Committee also signed the Brighton Declaration claiming the country "was fast developing a healthy environment to support women's participation in sports" (The Peninsular, 2013). The culmination of the Finland Secretariat was the IWG World Conference 2014 in Helsinki. They regarded this as a success, as it was well organised with 1,000 participants from 89 countries and all continents, and their success in connecting with so many International Federations meant they now knew "what IWG is and what we are doing, and what is important in the gender equality questions" (Mattila). The IOC president, Thomas Bach, was new in post at this time, and the IWG conference was one of his first meetings in that capacity and his first official engagement in Finland: "they said in the IOC that for several years he referred to the Helsinki Conference, and how important it is to get women and sport forward and gender equality" (Heinilä).

The IWG World Conference in 2014 marked 20 years since the establishment of the IWG as an outcome of the Brighton Conference in 1994. At the 2011 IWG Annual Meeting, the Finland Secretariat committed to setting up a working group with representatives of IWG, WSI, and IAPESGW to consider how to monitor progress on women and sport with a view to producing a Progress Report to mark the anniversary. In the IWG Annual Meeting in 2012, it was confirmed that the Anita White Foundation would undertake content analysis of the IWG Progress Reports from 1994 to 2010 (Matthews et al., 2012), and that these would be incorporated into a Brighton Plus Helsinki Progress Report. The purpose of this report was

> to compile a progress report which is intended to serve as a historical portrait of global developments in the women and sport movement from 1994 to the present day. Further that this progress report should be a source of inspiration for policy and decision makers world-wide who are working for advancing the status and opportunities for girls and women in sport.
> (International Working Group on Women and Sport, 2012)

The main findings of the Progress Report (Fasting et al., 2014) indicated that organisations in the African and Asian regions had been most active in implementing the principles of the Brighton Declaration, and women and sport organisations had the highest average in actions taken to promote gender equality in sports. Most organisations surveyed had taken action to increase the number of physically active women, include gender equality issues in training materials, and increase public knowledge about issues facing women's sport. The fewest actions that had been taken related to child-care provision, supporting retiring female athletes, addressing women's safety, particularly the prevention of eating disorders and injury protection, and the development of women in leadership positions.

The legacy of the IWG Finland Secretariat was to redraft the Brighton Declaration to the Brighton Plus Helsinki 2014 Declaration and an Action Plan. They described the original Brighton Declaration as an important document when contacting organisations and partners and indicated that they had a large number of signatories during their term, including Presidents of Federations and Paralympic Committees, along with Chairs of Women's and Gender Equality Committees. They advised that the International Sports Federations were keen to be involved and required more practical support. The revised Brighton Plus Helsinki 2014 Declaration states that it "embraces physical activity as an essential extension of organised sport, especially for girls and women. Hence, the Declaration includes reference to physical activity as well as sport, throughout" (International Working Group on Women and Sport, 2014). The revised Declaration also acknowledges in more detail the factors within and external to sport which affect women's levels of participation and locates the Declaration in the context of the United Nations Millenium (now Sustainable) Development Goals. The Declaration also draws on the recommendations from the IWG report on progress in the 20 years since the Brighton Conference (Fasting et al., 2014), recommending a need for mainstreaming, recognising the diversity of women and girls' needs across the lifespan, and the need for systematic research about women and sport.

Progress since 2014

One of the challenges that the IWG Finland Secretariat experienced was trying to improve the media coverage of women's sport. However, following their term hosting the IWG Secretariat, the National Council of Women of Finland launched a programme titled 100 Acts for Gender Equality in 2016. They worked systematically with the National Broadcasting Company of Finland, Yle, which gradually changed the coverage of men's and women's sports to be more equal. The Finnish media then started to evaluate their coverage of the number of articles and content of coverage for men and women.

The proactive approach by the IWG Finland Secretariat to connect with the European Union provided the foundations for a meeting with Androulla Vassiliou, who was the European Commissioner for Education, Culture, Youth, and Sports. In this meeting, they discussed the possibility of the European Union having recommendations on gender equality and sport, which was supported by Vassiliou. An EU Working Group on Gender Equality in Sport was established. Commissioner Vassiliou presented a recommendation at the IWG World Conference 2014 that a working group be established. This led to the formation of the European Commission's High Level Group on Gender Equality and Sport, supported by Finland, and in 2022 the publication of Recommendations and an Action Plan "Towards More Gender Equality and Sport" (European Union, 2022), with Heinilä serving as a member of the group.

In order to ensure their work was sustainable beyond their Secretariat, the Finnish team produced a booklet, which they handed over to the next IWG Secretariat in Botswana, 2014–2018. This included more clearly defining the structure and roles of the regional representatives on the IWG Group, as there were some difficulties in communicating with some of them. Heinilä continued as a co-opted member of the IWG Group during the Botswana term and had ongoing contacts with the Botswana Secretariat.

Looking Forward

When considering the future for gender issues and sport, Mattila and Heinilä reflected on the emergence of a strong anti-gender movement since their Secretariat, including the #MeToo movement, the impact of the Covid-19 pandemic on women, and issues of safety and violence against women, as well as human rights issues, including the impact on women of the Russian invasion of Ukraine.

In addition to addressing the anti-gender movement, the other priority area of focus going forward is identified as leadership in terms of providing pathways to help increase the numbers of women in leadership positions, the competence of sport leaders on gender equality issues, and diversity in sport leadership. They identified the importance of face-to-face meetings. The end of the IWG Finland Secretariat saw the IWG relocate to Botswana for the first time an African nation had hosted the Secretariat and the second World Conference on the continent.

Reference List

European Union. (2022). *Towards more gender equality and sport*. Publications Office of the European Union.

Fasting, K., Sand, T., Pike, E., & Matthews, J. (2014). *From Brighton to Helsinki: Women and sport progress report 1994–2014*. International Working Group on Women and Sport. www.iwginsighthub.org/iwg-leadership/resources

International Working Group on Women and Sport. (2012). *"From Brighton to Helsinki" reporting on the global development of progress for girls and women in sport, 1994–2014*. [Unpublished concept paper]. Anita White Collection: University of Chichester.

International Working Group on Women and Sport. (2014). *Brighton plus Helsinki 2014 declaration on women and sport*. IWG.

Matthews, J., Pike, E., & White, A. (2012). *Analysis and review of the international working group on women and sport progress reports 1994–2010*. Anita White Collection: University of Chichester.

The Peninsular. (2013, April 4 Thursday). *Qatar and IWG sign pact*. Anita White Collection: University of Chichester, p. 29.

White, A. (2010, August 26). *IWG issues past and present*. Paper presented for discussion. Anita White Collection: University of Chichester.

7 Determine the Future, Be Part of the Change, IWG Secretariat Botswana, 2014–2018

Interview with Dr Carole Oglesby and Game Mothibi

Introduction

Botswana assumed hosting rights for the IWG from 2014 to 2018, becoming the first African nation to host the Secretariat and the second to host the World Conference (following Namibia in 1998). They became the custodians of the updated Brighton Plus Helsinki 2014 Declaration, taking a threefold focus on issues for women and sport locally in Region 5 (Southern Africa), nationally in Africa, and globally for women and girls around the world.

Co-Chair and Secretary General: Dr Carole Oglesby and Game Mothibi

The co-Chairs for the IWG Botswana Secretariat were Ruth Maphorisa from Botswana and Carole Oglesby from the USA, with Game Mothibi serving as the Secretary General. Maphorisa served two terms as IWG co-Chair from 2014 to 2018 as the representative of the Botswana Secretariat, and then continuing during the term of the next Secretariat in New Zealand (NZ) from 2018 to 2022. Her background was in the Botswana government, serving as the Permanent Secretary in the Ministry of Youth, Sport, and Culture of Botswana and later as Director of the Department of Public Service Management. Oglesby became the other co-Chair responding to an advertisement when it became clear that the previous co-Chair, Raija Mattila, would not be continuing. This chapter is based on interviews with Oglesby and Mothibi, who responded positively to the invitation to be interviewed, and subsequent extensive correspondence with them.

Both Oglesby and Mothibi outlined the significance of their family backgrounds, and particularly the influence of their mothers on their future engagement with, and careers in, sport. Oglesby primarily participated in softball, while Mothibi's main sport was table tennis. Oglesby described herself as coming from

DOI: 10.4324/9781003356868-7
This chapter has been made available under a CC-BY 4.0 license.

a very sporting family. My dad was a really good baseball player so, in that sense, wasn't that unusual a man, because he was very sports oriented. But the more unusual part was my mother . . . she played high school basketball in the early 1930s, and her team got to the finals for the State of Oklahoma.

Mothibi explained how her mother experienced discrimination on the basis of gender in three ways as a church Minister: as a woman, as an unmarried woman, and as a woman who had children but was not married. Her mother became an activist: "trying to pave the way for women Priests who came after her because she managed to get in after really fighting hard and even lead the Church Synod; she was also the voice for women on this stage". Mothibi explained that this made her curious as to why the culture in her country and in the church meant there were different experiences for women like her mother, different prize money for men and women in her sport of table tennis, and the women and sport movement "helped me answer some of those questions". She was drawn to table tennis because she was quiet and shy, and she found the environment in this sport very supportive, without too many fans. She eventually moved into administration, founded the Women in Table Tennis organisation, which enabled her to attend the Women in Sport Botswana Conference, and successfully advocated for equal prize money for men and women in Table Tennis.

Oglesby's family moved to the Los Angeles area, where she played softball in national championships, going on to study physical education at UCLA. Here, "the PE women were dead set against high level competition because they thought it was exploitative and pulled too much focus away from what they thought was important, which was physical education for all, and community recreational sport". However, she described herself as "part of a whole generation of generational change" which was focused on ensuring that elite programmes were developed for women. She became the first president of the first organisation that sponsored collegiate championships for women in the USA and then became the representative for women's sport on the World University Games programme housed in the USA.

> I used to tell people that my job was to hand out socks and jocks because basically the men didn't give me anything to do other than the most menial, secretarial kind of tasks, but . . . I really learned a lot and one of the things I saw was the importance of the international system.

Through her international role, Oglesby met several women who were active in the international women and sport movement, including Anita White and Celia Brackenridge. During this time, she was involved in discussions regarding the hosting of an international event. When the Brighton Conference was announced, Oglesby explained,

> when the announcements hit about this big, new conference that was going to be held in Brighton, I was a combination of hurt and saddened that nobody from the US was involved, to my knowledge, in the planning of this conference. I felt like we were as forthcoming as we could be about our ideas.

For this, and other reasons, Oglesby did not attend the Brighton Conference. She did, however, recognise the value of IWG and attended several board meetings representing WomenSport International, IAPESGW, or the Americas region "and was and am completely committed to the IWG and the vision of the founders".

When it came to becoming the co-Chair for the IWG in Botswana, Oglesby explained how she drew on her sporting background to help with the role. She described how she was a utility player in softball, one who was not always the first choice for any given position but who had the knowledge and skills to play multiple roles if the first choice player was not able to continue to play. In the case of the IWG, the previous co-Chair, Mattila, did not continue in the new Secretariat, and so for Oglesby, "I look at my 4 years as the co-chair, as kind of like one of my latter day utility player things". Her background in softball also proved a meeting point with Ruth Maphorisa, the other co-Chair, also a softball player. Mothibi's role in the Botswana IWG Secretariat was more "hands on" in the day-to-day running of the Secretariat at the local level. She acknowledged the support of Oglesby and Anita White, who "helped me grow in my activism". In addition, Mothibi raised an issue experienced by many women, and one which has been consistently identified in IWG Progress Report, that of the need for childcare to enable her to fulfil her role. She reflected again on her own mother's support and activism:

> As I began my new role at the IWG office, I was met with the daunting reality that my daughter, who was just one year old at the time, would need to be cared for while I was away on business trips, working long hours and rarely home. Fortunately, my mother was an absolute godsend. With her unwavering support, she graciously took on the responsibility of caring for my daughter, allowing me to focus on my career without having to worry about my child's well-being. I will forever be grateful to my mother for her selflessness and dedication to our family.

Relationship of IWG with Other Organisations

The IWG Botswana Secretariat indicated that they had good support from the partners who had worked with the previous Secretariat in Finland, primarily from the European Union. In addition, they worked closely with the

Commonwealth Secretariat. Oglesby flagged the growing relationship with the United Nations at this time, which she described as "like another one of those, like the Olympic movement, very European oriented and to some extent a little bit colonialist". However, there was also support from The Association For International Sport for All (TAFISA) and other organisations which were keen to work in Africa. For example, Mothibi explained that they adopted some TAFISA programmes to promote physical activity, while TAFISA helped train the Botswana Sport Volunteer Movement volunteers and held their board meeting during the IWG conference to support that event.

Mothibi also explained the domestic support which she described as good but challenging. She was working for the Botswana National Sports Commission (BNSC), which hosted the IWG within the Ministry of Sport premises, seconded to the IWG for four years, for which she reported to the IWG Global Executive, and there was also a local organising committee for the IWG:

> So I had in total 5 structures to report to, and it was not easy, . . . the time that I take to write reports for each one of them, to have meetings with each of the structures, to satisfy all the structures, it was also time-consuming, and sometimes exhausting.

Some of the particular challenges related to having to report to different groups how funds were being used, and yet they were not helping with raising funds for the office and the conference. Mothibi outlined a number of clashes: where groups expected the IWG Secretariat to serve their needs and between the priorities of the Conference local organising committee and the IWG Secretariat and Board. A particular issue for Mothibi was working as a BNSC officer while "being an advocate for women and having to question BNSC policies and procedures, which created clashes with some of the operational procedures of the Commission and what the IWG stood for".

Both Mothibi and Oglesby discussed the differences and overlaps in the work being carried out by the different international women and sport groups, including the IWG, IAPESGW, and WomenSport International, which existed during the term of their Secretariat, and the Global Observatory for Gender Equality and Sport, which has been established since then. This led Mothibi to reflect on how the various women and sport organisations are "working in silos", with confusion about who was leading on particular themes, questioning "how much resource and capacity" there is for all of the organisations, and how this leads to confusion with "people asking is there any tension within the global movement, who is the boss?" Oglesby also picked up on this, recommending that this is

> something that we need to be vigilant about and try to respect one another, try to do the boundary work that keeps us all feeling like we're helping one another out and not getting in the way of one another.

IWG Secretariat, 2014–2018

The bid for Botswana to host the IWG from 2014 to 2018 was written by Mothibi in her role as project officer for the Botswana Sports Commission, where she had a remit for women in sport. Initially, she felt "that it was too much for my country" but was encouraged by IWG Global Executive members and the Finland Secretariat to apply. The Botswana Minister called her to ask what benefit there was to the country hosting the IWG, and Mothibi explained that she had to be clear that there were no financial benefits and so needed to highlight that this would enable them to promote Botswana to the rest of the world. "And then I managed to get all the support from some of the organisations, and from the ministry". She explained that prior to being awarded the hosting rights

> we didn't see the level or how big is this thing we were hosting, you know, it's one thing to say we are going to host this. . . . We did not really realise that this is quite a big responsibility for the country until we woke up when we got the hosting.

Mothibi reflected on the fact that, prior to hosting the IWG, gender issues were viewed as a side issue from the main sports system:

> We had a movement, we had women who were making a noise around the women in sport movement, but those issues were just talking, they are not necessarily infiltrated into the day to day running of sport councils and the day to day running of sports in general. So, we managed to make sure that the gender mainstreaming happens in Botswana.

One of the outcomes of hosting the IWG was women in sports being included in central sports policy:

> There's a gender in sport framework now . . . at that time there was an ongoing review of the Sports Act in Botswana, and now the Act recognises Women in Sport Botswana, there's a seat for women in the BNSC Board, there's language within the act that talks to gender equality.

More broadly, Mothibi described how the IWG Botswana created conversations around gender equality issues:

> I remember there was an issue of gender-based violence within the sport sector, school sports, and IWG was the first to make a statement and then we were also the first to make follow ups, and because of that people were really rallying behind us.

Hosting the IWG also encouraged more women to take up leadership positions, with many of them supported to train for leadership:

I remember for the first time within Botswana there was a full 7 women who campaigned as a team for the Botswana National Olympic Committee (BNOC) elections . . . . I knew that there was going to be a lot of backlash as it was an all women campaign group but it had to be done to shake things . . . we ended with only one woman from the group who managed to go into the board at that time, but it's left a long-lasting legacy in Botswana increasing women's representation to 42%, and people are now not afraid to go for elections. And right now, there are 57% women on the BNOC board . . . more than 60% remain on the board.

Oglesby's involvement with the IWG Botswana Secretariat came later, once Mothibi and Maphorisa had put together the core team. She described "a pretty intensive experience" of visiting Botswana to meet the team and agree on the tasks for each person, and felt that the Botswana Secretariat was really successful in securing corporate sponsorship and media coverage, progressing in "an intense way". For Oglesby, the Botswana programme was "exceptional in relation to bringing in persons of colour, women of colour, from all around the globe". She outlined the primary focus of the IWG Botswana Secretariat as threefold: Africa, Region 5 (Southern Africa), and the diaspora of women of colour around the world. Oglesby highlighted, in particular, the challenges for women in Africa of raising issues around sexual harassment and abuse, which she felt they did "with quite a lot of courage . . . I thought they were understanding". Oglesby's reference to "courage" was addressed by Mothibi, who explained that issues related to athletes who identify as transgender, intersex, or Differences in Sex Development (DSD) came to the fore during their term. World Athletics asked the IWG Botswana Secretariat to remove the session on this topic from their World Conference, but Mothibi "was adamant that we need to do this for Women's movement", and a session including Caster Semenya took place, which she felt provided a voice for this issue which is continuing beyond the IWG Botswana Secretariat.

The IWG Progress Report for this Secretariat demonstrated that the respondents to the survey had been very active in improving the situation for women and girls, particularly in terms of increased opportunities to be physically active. The report recommended that more attention needs to be given to increasing the number of women in decision-making positions, prevention of gender-based violence, increasing the coverage and improving the portrayal of women in sports in the media, and undertaking research on girls and women in sport so that all policy is evidence-based (Fasting et al., 2018). The legacy of the IWG Botswana Secretariat was The Botswana Big 5 (International Working Group on Women and Sport, 2018). This was a play on wildlife safaris in the region, but highlighting the need for gender mainstreaming with five priority areas, each symbolised by an animal: Media (rhino), Accountability (lion), Representation (leopard), Research to practice (buffalo), Communication (elephant).

Progress since 2018

In order to achieve the three regional legacies of the IWG Botswana Secretariat (local to Region 5, continental for Africa, and international), Mothibi explained that they held an Africa Conference, which raised the issues happening for the women and sport movement in Africa, and supported organisations to develop initiatives in their own countries. She identified particular success in Africa, mainly because the IWG Secretariat was invited to the African Union Sports Commission meetings throughout their term, which enabled them to share with sports ministers what was happening for women and girls in Africa.

In contrast, Mothibi felt less was achieved internationally in the short term, but that the impact may be felt in the longer term. However, they were successful in developing the relationships with the United Nations, Commonwealth, The Association For International Sport for All (TAFISA), and also Asia Women in Sports, where she saw commonalities with the experiences of women in Africa:

> That is why it was easy for Asia to come alive during the IWG Women in Sport when it was in Africa. But in terms of Europe and America I don't think we made impact, but we made a lot of relationships between European organisations and with American organisations that I hope they will definitely be helping IWG going forward.

Oglesby also spoke to the number of organisations that are now working in the women and sport space, which she described as

> chaotic... a big mess... I think there must be some way where the leadership at the international level would point the way for pathways that would encourage organisations having their sphere of operation, but having them also see that there are boundaries, and we have to be aware of and respectful of one another's boundaries, and work together to negotiate whatever boundary problems come to be.

She identified, in particular, the Global Observatory for Gender Equality and Sport, which is "a new baby on the one hand, but it also has an enormous potential bandwidth".

Looking Forward

When asked to outline what they felt were the key issues facing the international women and sport movement, and specifically the IWG, going forward, both Mothibi and Oglesby talked about the importance of having a voice to influence global trends. Mothibi was particularly concerned that women in Africa lost their voice following the IWG Botswana Secretariat's term of hosting, and "we need to bring that voice back, because with that voice we're making an impact". Oglesby made a call for evidence-based advocacy and, specifically, for the academics in the IWG "to work in the real world" rather than being "some high flown academic community that only talks to each other". This was identified by Mothibi as a particular challenge in Africa because

> we don't have a lot of researchers within the Africa women and sport movement . . . we want that to come up, because that is the only way that can actually help the IWG to base their work plan from data driven agenda from Africa . . . We have a lot of programmes happening on the ground. We want you to hear our stories.

Mothibi expressed her concerns about "tokenism in the women and sport movement", stating:

> I don't want to sit in a panel because I'm a black African woman, and we need it to balance the demographics there, I want to be there because you feel like whatever I'm going to say, it's going to contribute to the discussion.

She argued that the IWG needs to sit down with people from the Global South

> and really understand what we really need, what plans we have for Africa and for Asia and for South America. I'm not saying Europe and America are good enough, but . . . I don't want Europe and America to decide on the agenda for women in sport without Africa and Asia at the table. I want all the women from the groups to decide on the agenda.

In order to achieve this, Mothibi is working with the GIZ (the German Development Agency) on developing a network of 100 organisations in Africa that have a focus on Sport for Development and gender equality and also organising an Africa Conference in 2025. As a specific example of this, Mothibi outlined the challenges for Africa, such as dependence on digital communication, including access to the IWG Insight Hub and online registration systems for the IWG conferences, advising that the IWG needs "to understand the stories from the most difficult backgrounds and accommodate them" to be truly global and inclusive.

Both Mothibi and Oglesby proposed that the signatories of the Brighton Declaration should be reporting on the work that they are doing "that advances the role and status of women in sport in your country" (Oglesby). Mothibi described the Declaration as "a good Bible for us" but also felt that "we don't have any mechanism to follow up after the signing to say 'what has been done' except through the progress report. But how many people respond to the progress reports?" She felt there was an urgent need to measure the impact of signing the Declaration "which is currently lacking". Mothibi's view was that connecting the IWG network should be the main priority going forward: "We need the network to continue the work, to continue communicating and disseminating information on women in sport, and to continue advocating activism".

There was an interesting difference of opinion between the IWG Botswana co-Chair and Secretary General about the significance of issues related to gender identity. Oglesby suggested these were likely to be "heavily debated" and "fraught" for IWG going forward. However, Mothibi suggested that while this is

> a very important topic for the Europeans, I can tell you the truth. It is the least of our priorities in Africa within the sports movement. We have socioeconomic issues to deal with. We have racism within sport, within women in sport to deal with, and we will talk about transgender, we appreciate it is a very important topic. But it's not a priority for Africa.

For Mothibi, the most important issue that needs to be addressed by the IWG is racism in sports:

> There is racism inside the women and sport movement. We're saying that there's racism in sport that is affecting women. . . . We want racism to be part of the conversation that we are not afraid to confront and talk about as much.

Mothibi explained that, if there was one change she could make for the IWG, it is that

> I want Africa to be in the global movement. I want Asia to be in the global movement . . . also the movement should be able to go where it's difficult to go into. I know Africa was difficult because of lack of resources and cultural issues, but it's something that we can't run away from. I know Asia is very difficult, because they are too timid and very quiet on women and sport issues, they don't want these gender inequalities happening in their sport to be exposed but we need to do something about that.

Oglesby added that she believes

> it is crucial we maintain the centrepiece of our work as 'women in all their diversity', including ensuring there is diversity in the countries represented on the Global Executive. It is women who continue to be discriminated against, harassed, abused, ignored, silenced, all on the basis of race, gender identity, age, socio-economic status, disability. We have a long way to go to bring equality to women in all their diversity.

The experiences of the black Botswanan Secretary General, and the white American co-Chair of the IWG Botswana Secretariat, highlight the opportunities and challenges of a global movement which needs to give equal value to all voices, not be afraid to have difficult conversations, while negotiating tensions and backlash from within and without the immediate Secretariat. Mothibi and Oglesby drew on their sporting backgrounds as utility players and daughters of women who had fought for gender equality in their own lives, to leave a legacy of "The Big 5" from their term of office.

Reference List

Fasting, K., Pike, E., Matthews, J., & Sand. T. (2018). *From Helsinki to Gaborone: IWG Progress report 2013–2018*. International Working Group on Women and Sport. www.iwginsighthub.org/iwg-leadership/resources
International Working Group on Women and Sport. (2018). *Botswana Big 5*. https://iwgwomenandsport.org/wp-content/uploads/2020/09/IWG-Botswana-Big-5-Legacy.pdf

8 Change Inspires Change, IWG Secretariat New Zealand, 2018–2022

Interview with Rachel Froggatt

Introduction

The IWG Secretariat from 2018 to 2022 was hosted by New Zealand (NZ). The local co-Chair was Raewyn Lovett, with Ruth Maphorisa as the previous co-Chair from Botswana continuing to serve during this term. Lovett remained as co-Chair for the following Secretariat, 2022–2026. Professionally, she is a lawyer, practising in commercial and corporate law, with an extensive background in sports governance. She served as Chair of Netball New Zealand for seven years, receiving the Officer of the New Zealand Order of Merit for her service in 2015. Following terms on the boards of Sport New Zealand Ihi Aotearoa (Sport NZ) and High Performance Sport New Zealand (HPSNZ), she became their Chair in 2023. It was not possible to reach either of the co-Chairs to be interviewed for this book, but the Secretary General, Rachel Froggatt, took part in an interview and extensive correspondence. This IWG term witnessed the global Covid-19 pandemic, which impacted on the capacity of the Secretariat to participate in global meetings in person, and national lockdowns meant the planned World Conference was delayed by six months in order to facilitate international delegates. The Secretariat had to move quickly to an online way of operating, a hybrid conference, and enhanced digital platforms, providing the foundations for the IWG to consider how it would have "mana" (the Maori word for power and status) in a post-pandemic world.

Secretary General: Rachel Froggatt

Froggatt is a New Zealander with more than 20 years experience working in commercial sport. She started her career with an internship in a sports marketing firm in Australia. She moved from there to the UK to work full-time in Formula One for nearly four years. Here, she described how she became

> disillusioned with big brand international commercial sports . . . it's just such a big beast, and it just swallows everything in front of it, and you

DOI: 10.4324/9781003356868-8
This chapter has been made available under a CC-BY 4.0 license.

become quite tired and burnt out. And I started questioning the purpose about what I was doing.

After a period travelling, she returned to the UK to work in a sports media PR agency before moving to Germany to work as a director of sponsorship for a European advertising agency. In this role, she attended major sports events, including the London 2012 Paralympic Games, where she "was just completely blown away by it, just the idea that sport could be used as a platform to change societal views of people, improve the situation of underprivileged groups". She made the decision to return to NZ as the commercial and marketing director for the New Zealand Paralympic team in late 2014, ensuring investment into Paralympic sport for the Games in Rio 2016 and PyeongChang in 2018.

Froggatt explained that she had no intention of leaving this role when startup organisation Women in Sport Aotearoa (WISPA, Ngā Wāhine Hākinakina o Aotearoa) advertised for a Chief Executive who would also serve as the Secretary General of the IWG, 2018–2022. She felt that she had to "put myself forward for this, like what a phenomenal opportunity to build an organisation from scratch, and to be part of an international movement like this, I would really regret if I don't try". She started the role in September 2018, which meant she had never experienced an IWG World Conference, and was then expected to lead on the planning for the one in 2022. Ten days after her appointment, the Botswana Secretariat arrived in Auckland to hand over the Secretariat. They had two and a half days to try to learn everything they needed to take on hosting the IWG:

> it was quite overwhelming at the beginning I'll be honest, because, the best description I ever heard of this is one of my board members said in a meeting once: we have to remember that what we did was take this ginormous international beast and drop it on the head of a teeny, tiny barely breathing baby of an organisation and go 'here, do this'. So, you know we set ourselves up quite a challenge at the beginning.

She reflected on this as a recurrent challenge for the IWG that the change in Secretariat each quadrennial meant the IWG effectively "went to sleep" while the new Secretariat came to understand their role and how to deliver.

Relationship of IWG with Other Organisations

The IWG NZ Secretariat was a direct initiative of WISPA. The organisation was founded in 2016 by Julie Paterson and Sarah Leberman, both of whom had been working on different women and sport professional development programmes in the USA and returned to NZ committed to setting up a national organisation. They located 22 foundation members with a deliberate balance of white and Māori representatives and asked them one question: "do you think the New Zealand sports sector will achieve equity for women and girls by itself or do you think it needs an intervention?" The members agreed that an intervention was needed, but, at the time, WISPA was

> a teeny, tiny, volunteer organisation, with no money and no resource, the only organisation in the whole country that had an interest in achieving equity for women and girls . . . very much on their own at the very beginning.

However, there were two significant developments for WISPA. The first was a decision to bid to host the IWG "because they needed a focal point, and they needed something that you know everyone could rally around and invest their time and energy into to start creating the kind of waves they wanted to create within the sector". The bid secured significant government support, including from Sport New Zealand, Auckland Unlimited, the Ministry of Business, Innovation, and Employment, the Ministry of Foreign Trade, the Ministry for Women, and the New Zealand Olympic Committee. They flew a group to the IWG World Conference 2018 in Botswana, where they were advised that they had won the bid, giving them only five months to prepare to host. The second significant development was a change in the NZ government from centre-right to centre-left policies, and a new Minister for Sport and Recreation, the Hon Grant Robertson. Under his leadership, Sport New Zealand's focus changed to a more inclusive approach, which included the development of a strategy for sport for women and girls and a commitment to support the IWG.

Froggatt also explained a strategic approach to connecting their stakeholders with the world conference by presenting it as a focal point that

> we've got the entire world arriving on our doorstep and, at the time of May 2022, we have to stand on the stage and say that we are amongst the best in the world, and we are not at the moment so we've got a lot of work to do between now and that four year window.

There was also a government decision to bid to host major women's sports events, and they secured the rights to host the ICC Women's Cricket World Cup, the Rugby World Cup, and (in partnership with Australia) the FIFA Women's World Cup, all during the term of the IWG NZ Secretariat. Froggatt built relationships with the leaders of each of these tournaments, all of whom were women, and between the four of them, they would take part in joint speaking engagements and extensive information sharing, presenting the IWG and the three major events as "The Big Four". Each of the events was affected by the pandemic with postponements, but the support of the government and Sport New Zealand meant they invested resource into ensuring the events still went ahead.

In particular, the IWG World Conference had to be postponed by six months, as the original date meant that there would be no international delegates due to border closings and lockdown restrictions. The move to a hybrid event was also challenging as "IWG had never been sold virtually before, we didn't know how much people would buy into that, so there was a lot of uncertainty". These challenges were eased by the fact that the incoming IWG Secretariat had been agreed a year earlier than usual, based on the IWG NZ's experiences of having had such a short turnaround from the Botswana Secretariat, which had an unintended consequence that

> we were able to build a team kind of approach with the UK. You know that we were in partnership with each other. And so, when we had to say to the UK guys hey, listen, we have to postpone, it's a really shit situation, this is what's going on, if we hadn't had that relationship it would have been very difficult for us to argue for that, because we knew that we were in pushing ourselves into their Secretariat period, because they were supposed to start on the first of October, and we were doing it in November.

The postponement also meant that the IWG UK Secretariat team were appointed and able to attend the IWG World Conference 2022 and learn from the IWG NZ Secretariat

The IWG World Conference 2022 also enabled the Secretariat to develop other strategic relationships. Froggatt specifically mentioned the improved relationship with, and support of, the IOC in contrast to those outlined by previous Secretariats. And the IWG NZ Secretariat had a strategic focus on the Pacific Islands. They worked with the Australian Department for Foreign Affairs and Trade, creating three Pacific Hubs in Fiji, Samoa, and Papua New Guinea. During the World Conference, leaders engaged with the online programme and did their own activities alongside the conference, enabling those who could not afford, or did not have the opportunity to attend in person, to still access the Conference. It is notable that this was a recommendation of a report presented to the IWG UK/Namibia Secretariat in 1996, in which Australian IWG member Darlison (1996) noted the formation of the Sport Pacific Islands Network of Sportswomen (SPINS) who would be seeking representation on the IWG with a strong view that the South Pacific should not be represented through Australia or NZ due to their "residual colonial status in the Pacific".

IWG Secretariat, 2018–2022

Froggatt explained that the WISPA Strategic Plan included a direct statement regarding the IWG which informed the activities of the Secretariat. There were four pillars to this plan which included using evidence to challenge the system; increasing representation of women in sports leadership; women and girls having a powerful and respected voice; and a pillar dedicated to the IWG's legacy and how to improve the IWG. This was going well with what Froggatt described as "momentum coming into the sector and internationally women's sport was on the rise" until March 2020 when the first Covid-19 lockdown was implemented and "all of sport completely collapsed and nothing was happening". This created particular challenges for commercial sports which were losing money from a lack of fan engagement and broadcasting rights, "but all of the hysteria was attached to men's sport . . . it's like women are invisible. It was so shocking".

As a response to this, the IWG launched a programme, Leadership from Lockdown which was a 45-minute curated conversation each week asking leaders from NZ and global sport to discuss the challenges they were facing, but ensuring the discussions included what was happening for women's sport and athletes. The NZ government launched a recovery package for sport, and Sport New Zealand included criteria that funding would only be given to applications that included support for women's sport. Froggatt reflected on whether the pandemic and the particular impact on women's sport actually frustrated and offended so many people so much

> that it actually supercharged the movement. So actually, they fought harder and longer to get those programmes back up and didn't accept any shit from people about 'oh we don't have the money, and we don't have the time, we don't have the resource' . . . people like a fight back from women within the system and it was amazing to watch.

She referred to subsequent international women's sport tournaments which had record-breaking audiences.

One of the strategic priorities that the IWG NZ Secretariat was able to progress was the development of an Insight Hub which was part of their original Strategic Plan. They were keen to have a legacy that would be sustainable by the incoming Secretariat without significant resource implications and able to move to a different country, learning from previous Secretariats such as Australia, whose Sydney Scoreboard proved too challenging for subsequent Secretariats to maintain. In addition, they wanted to develop something that could be delivered in parallel by WISPA as a regional hub focused on Oceania case studies. It was particularly important for them that the Hub contained recordings of the 2022 World Conference so that content could be made widely available, something that became even more apparent during the conference when in-person sessions that weren't being recorded were over-crowded because people prioritised attending those knowing they could watch recorded sessions later. This resulted in a last-minute decision to record all sessions with unplanned additional costs. However, on balance, Froggatt said that the need to postpone and then deliver a hybrid conference because of the Covid-19 restrictions ended up being really powerful, and she was even pleased with the conference venue following a need to relocate when the planned venue for the conference burned down early in their term as the Secretariat.

A key driving force for the IWG NZ Secretariat was to modernise the IWG itself. Froggatt described it as "a fairly traditional entity, functioning in a fairly traditional way", including lengthy reports and newsletters that were unlikely to be read. In particular, they were keen

> to move IWG from having quite a big focus on the academic community when it came to us, and we wanted to shift it to become a much more action orientated organisation focused on sports leaders. So, we put enormous amounts of energy into building relationships like IOC, International Paralympic Committee, Commonwealth Games Federation, International Federations and in New Zealand the national sports organisations because we felt like, to be an advocacy entity and to be successful, we need to be influencing the people that had the money and the power to make change.

They were particularly keen to engage more men with the organisation, something that they struggled with, in particular "we couldn't convince men that they would be safe and welcome at the conference". For NZ, there was also a specific focus on their indigenous programme which culminated in a separate Indigenous Statement on Call to Action (Women in Sport Aotearoa, 2022).

The Secretariat invested in IWG branding and a website, so that each new Secretariat did not have to spend time re-inventing these. She also identified the challenge of the IWG database – the IWG NZ Secretariat received an excel spreadsheet of approximately 7,000 names and emails, with duplication and missing information. They had intended to introduce a proper customer relationship management system including contact information and details of when they had signed the Brighton Declaration, which conferences they had attended, and a structured communications methodology. This was impacted by the pandemic and the IWG NZ Secretariat were unable to progress this as much as they had wished, which also made it more challenging for them to attract delegates to attend their conference.

Froggatt raised an issue which recurred through most Secretariats, which related to the challenge of the IWG not being a constituted organisation and so having to report to multiple stakeholders including the WISPA board, the IWG Global Executive, the government and commercial funders among others. She explained that what was really challenging was

> the amount of voices and the amount of opinions . . . I found the reporting requirements to be really onerous, and I think I spent way more time reporting and keeping stakeholders happy than was reasonable for the size of our organisation and the size of the job at hand.

The IWG 2022 Progress Report (Cockburn & Atkinson, 2022) highlighted a number of ongoing barriers to equity, including gendered social, cultural, and religious norms, lack of women in leadership roles, and media coverage. The report also flagged emerging issues for consideration, including intersectional gender identities, motherhood, disability, and the impact of Covid-19. The 2022 World Conference concluded with a Call to Action, with the separate Indigenous Statement, and the Aotearoa Legacy (International Working Group on Women and Sport, 2022), which outlines 10 Global Legacies of the Secretariat, including improved digital infrastructure, Insight Hub, collaboration and connections, and commitment to indigeneity.

Progress since 2022

This book was written one year following the end of the IWG NZ Secretariat, and so there was limited time to demonstrate what impact hosting the IWG had had or what progress there had been since the end of their term. Froggatt did reflect on the strength of the "family ties" of those involved in the IWG, but also the challenge that the decision-makers in sport are still primarily middle-aged white men who "could just easily ignore us". She described their deliberate strategy to move beyond the IWG's tendency "to be quite inward facing", to engage with those in sports organisations who could "start to push change upwards through to governance and into leadership". For example, in 2019, the IWG joined forces with WSI and IAPESGW to write a letter sharing their "collective view" of "great disappointment in the decision taken by the International Association of Athletics Federations (IAAF) to restrict testosterone levels in female runners", referencing the Brighton Declaration's principle to comply with international charters (International Working Group on Women and Sport, 2019). She felt that the IWG probably had "more mana" since the 2022 World Conference as a result of engaging people globally through the conference.

Froggatt reflected on the relevance of the Brighton Plus Helsinki 2014 Declaration, expressing her concerns that "you sign it and then you never hear from us again". She felt that there should be regular correspondence with signatories with a dedicated area of the website or Insight Hub. This related to the need for the improved customer database. It also created problems for those collecting data for the Progress Report as it was challenging to contact people, and then those who were contacted felt that they were only engaged with every four years to provide content for the Report. Towards the end of the IWG NZ Secretariat, the United Nations (UN) developed their own Sport for Generation Equality charter, which Froggatt felt "had more funding behind it and could be quite a problem as a competitor to IWG". Her view was that there was significant potential for the Brighton Declaration if it was modernised to a customer engagement programme, which would also make it easier to sell the conference as the logical place for signatories to meet every four years.

Looking Forward

Froggatt considered whether the IWG should change its name from Women in Sport to Gender Equality in Sport to move it away from sounding like a women's conference on a women's issue. Such rebranding might help modernise and also make the IWG feel more inclusive and relevant to everyone:

> Don't underestimate the power of people like wanting to feel safe in an environment. If they're fearful that they're going to arrive and be criticized... a lot of really good men stayed away because, ... it's counterproductive for a man to lead a solution for a woman.

She also reflected on the relationship with other international women and sport organisations, such as WomenSport International and IAPESGW, describing relations in the early days of their Secretariat as "a bit disconnected". She felt, by the end of their Secretariat, the relationship between the groups was healthy but that this had required time agreeing and showing respect for other organisations, their histories and different areas of specialism:

> We just always saw ourselves as, in Māori its kaitiaki, it's a guardian. So, we saw ourselves as a guardian of IWG for a period of 4 years, we didn't own it, it didn't belong to us and then we were passing it on. So, it's like growing a plant, you know, you take it, you feed it, you water it, you help it grow, and then you pass it on to a new owner and hope they don't kill it.

Reference List

Cockburn, R., & Atkinson, L. (2002). *The international working group on women and sport 2022 progress report*. International Working Group on Women and Sport. www.iwginsighthub.org/iwg-leadership/resources

Darlison, E. (1996, June 3). *Facsimile to Andy Hansen*. Anita White Collection: University of Chichester.

International Working Group on Women and Sport. (2019, May 20). *Letter to international association of athletics federations*. Anita White Collection: University of Chichester.

International Working Group on Women and Sport. (2022). *The Aotearoa legacy*. https://iwgwomenandsport.org/wp-content/uploads/2023/05/The-Aotearoa-Legacy.pdf

Women in Sport Aotearoa. (2022). *The Aotearoa legacy*. Women in Sport Aotearoa.

9 Share the Change, IWG Secretariat United Kingdom, 2022–2026

Interview with Annamarie Phelps and Lisa O'Keefe

Introduction

The IWG Secretariat moved from New Zealand (NZ) to the United Kingdom (UK) in 2022, marking the first time that the IWG has returned to a former host country. The two Secretariats worked closely together in the year prior to the handover in order to navigate the challenges of the Covid-19 pandemic and the postponement of the 2022 IWG World Conference. This meant the handover took place prior to the conference for the first time in the IWG's history, and the UK was already hosting the Secretariat when NZ held its conference, illustrating the flexible governance processes on which the IWG is established. The IWG UK's World Conference will take place in 2026 with a theme yet to be confirmed at the time of writing this book, but the theme for the UK's bid to host the IWG 2022–2026 was #sharethechange.

Co-Chair and Secretary General: Annamarie Phelps CBE OLY and Lisa O'Keefe

The IWG UK's co-Chair was Annamarie Phelps, with the former NZ co-Chair Raewyn Lovett continuing during this Secretariat. Lovett did not respond to invitations to be interviewed, but an interview was conducted with Phelps along with the IWG UK's Secretary General Lisa O'Keefe.

Phelps and O'Keefe both have backgrounds as high-performance athletes: Phelps as a former Olympic and World Champion rower and O'Keefe as former Scotland rugby international. Neither Phelps nor O'Keefe had planned to have careers in the women and sport movement – indeed, Phelps explicitly said that she had "tried to avoid the women's sport movement through most of my career . . . I really didn't want to be seen as just fighting for the women". Phelps read geography at university and progressed to have a career as an art dealer. O'Keefe studied business and worked as a stockbroker while playing rugby, until a serious injury encouraged her to rethink her career pathway and, while recuperating from her injury, she undertook a postgraduate degree in sport.

DOI: 10.4324/9781003356868-9
This chapter has been made available under a CC-BY 4.0 license.

Both Phelps and O'Keefe outlined experiences which took them on a pathway addressing gender inequalities in sport and ultimately leading the IWG Secretariat, 2022–2026. Phelps had been a member of the Women's Sports Foundation (now Women in Sport), where she was exposed to a number of the issues confronted by women in sport. In her second year in the national women's rowing team, she was elected as the lightweight women's athletes representative to work with the governing body to resolve any issues they were experiencing. She explained that

> I learnt really quickly to communicate our issues as something that could benefit the whole team. . . . So, rather than saying, it's not fair that we don't get that, I'd say, why are you not investing in women's sport when we've got these medals, and we don't have anything like equal support. . . . The medal table doesn't define between men and women, we could be doing better as a team, as a country if we capitalised on our successes.

Phelps went on to represent the open weight and lightweight women athletes, then became the rowing representative on the British Olympic Association Athlete Commission, before chairing the Women's Rowing Commission when she retired. During this period, Phelps became frustrated that women rowers were content to use equipment that had been designed for men and felt that they needed a different way to develop women's rowing. She was instrumental in dissolving the Women's Rowing Commission so that all issues were mainstreamed, "and that left me then not having to worry about the women in sport movement side of things so much and to focus on the development of British Rowing and its governance", eventually becoming the Chair of British Rowing. She was appointed Commander of the Order of the British Empire (CBE) in 2016 for services to rowing.

O'Keefe recognised the sporting opportunity made available to her through a private education, and it was not until a serious ACL injury that she experienced a catalogue of inequalities from being a female rugby international without the sort of medical care and support available to her male counterparts. She explained that "I've carried that with me ever since", and this led to a career change when she applied to work for the Women's Sports Foundation. Here, she "was a 5 foot 10 inch Scottish Rugby player who was pretty angry . . . but I would channel that positively . . . I really cared about trying to help people see inequalities and think differently". She briefly moved to the National Coaching Foundation before progressing to work at Sport England, where she learned

> a lot about how inequalities manifest themselves . . . about the importance of going into communities and genuinely listening to their experiences and challenges . . . I was getting the opportunity to see and understand the manifestation of the inequalities within sport. I didn't have the lived

experience of some of the settings, but I understood the feeling of difference, and not being treated correctly, and being let down by the sports system.

In her extensive career at Sport England, O'Keefe became an Executive Director, leading on governance reform, insight, and behaviour change, expertise that she brought into her role when successfully applying to become the Secretary General of the IWG in 2022.

Phelps had also started to focus more on gender equality issues when she joined the European Olympic Committees (EOC), chairing the Gender Equality, Diversity and Inclusion Commission where "with the European perspective you suddenly realise how much there is still to do across all sports". She described experiences in other European countries where it was not possible to discuss gender issues:

> On one occasion I was asked, why would a woman want to work in sport? Because they'll never be as good as men at sports and you couldn't possibly ever be taken seriously as a woman in sport. And these beliefs can be so ingrained, culturally . . . that you have to be careful to give the women in those countries the confidence to understand how to progress, and build on that equality rather than trying to shoot them to the top, which would be a really fragile position if they don't have the foundations and the support behind them . . . each country will have a different solution and a different way of addressing its challenges in terms of recognising and appreciating the contribution of women to sport.

Despite this, it was not Phelps' intention to apply to be the co-Chair of the IWG UK as she already had roles on the EOC and IOC Commissions. However, she was persuaded that her experience, connections, and roles would be valuable, having been commissioned to write a report of the 2018 Botswana Conference for UK Sport; and "my arm was twisted" into submitting an application and subsequently being appointed as the co-Chair along with Lovett, who continued from the previous Secretariat.

Relationship of IWG with Other Organisations

The IWG UK's Secretariat is hosted by the Sport and Recreation Alliance, formerly known as the Central Council of Physical Recreation (CCPR). It is significant to note that, while the Brighton Conference in 1994 is widely recognised as the first World Conference on Women and Sport, the CCPR had previously organised an International Conference on Women and Sport in 1978. It is reported that there were 163 delegates from 28 countries in attendance, including representatives of the IOC and Council of Europe, gathered to understand the way that contemporary sport treats women. There is limited documented evidence of any recommendations from the conference meaning "little traction was gained" (Matthews, 2020, p. 3) at the time. But the CCPR, under its new name of the Sport and Recreation Alliance, played a key role in the UK bidding for, and hosting, the IWG Secretariat from 2022 to 2026. Additional support is provided by the funders: Sport England, UK Sport, sportscotland, and Sport Wales; the University of Hertfordshire funding the IWG research activities; the City of London offering venues for IWG events.

O'Keefe identified the significance of the relationship with multiple national partners, including governing bodies, sports councils, voluntary organisations, and cities, where she felt the IWG could "create a spark, create an opportunity, and set it free so that they can use it in their part of the sports system and create that cultural and structural change". She extended this to the Global Executive, who could help them understand the systems and organisations in other countries and how the IWG can support work internationally.

For Phelps, it was also key that the IWG UK worked with International Sports Federations as these "are the ones that can intervene to create change to really make a difference to the way women experience sports. The International Federations drive the culture in their sport which influences the national federations which influences clubs and grassroots sports". She also felt that National Olympic Committees (NOCs) could be applying for IOC funding to drive programmes at the national level, which could support organised grassroots sport.

> But I think if we're talking genuinely globally about participation for women to keeping them active and healthy then you can't not work with the likes of UN and UNESCO, and regional bodies such as Council of Europe, because they can influence the politicians who more often than not fund NOCs. So, there is this enormous ecosystem . . . and those are the people that can . . . use these things as good stories for themselves if they wanted, if they were doing good things.

IWG Secretariat, 2022–2026

When the UK initially considered bidding to host the IWG, Phelps indicated that potential funders such as Sport England and UK Sport pushed the bid team to identify and clearly articulate the potential impact of a UK bid, particularly given that they were already investing in a number of women and sport organisations. This is a recurrent theme through each Secretariat: the relocation to a different host country every four years requires convincing new funders to invest and creates some instability in the governance and operations of the IWG. Phelps made the argument in the UK that

> there's no cohesive strategy around women in sports. All the organisations are doing brilliant stuff, but they're haven't been joined up historically and it would be much more effective and more efficient use of public money if actually, we work together on this. So, here is a fantastic opportunity book

ended by some amazing women's sports events in this 4-year period when we could try and raise the profile of women's sport.

She noted, in particular, the Commonwealth Games 2022 in Birmingham, which is where the handover event from NZ took place and is the venue for the 2026 IWG World Conference.

The Sport and Recreation Alliance contracted Elizabeth Pike as a consultant to lead on the bid writing. The bid Steering Committee was constituted of 30 individuals representing governmental and non-governmental agencies, including sports bodies, women's groups, the media, and academics. There were approximately 150 supporting organisations and ambassadors, and 35 letters of support in the final bid book. Both Phelps and O'Keefe reflected on the fact that the bid was written during the Covid-19 pandemic with all its challenges, but that the pandemic, while damaging, also helpfully exposed the fragility of women's sport and the need for this to be addressed, enabling large-scale consultations in the enforced virtual way of working.

The IWG UK's Strategic Plan, 2022–2026, focuses on three priorities: Connections, where the pace and impact of change is enhanced through connected and collaborative networks; Insight, driving a research and insight-led approach to gender equality; and Leadership and Advocacy, influencing policy and strategy through demonstrating the value and impact of systemic gender equality. For O'Keefe, she felt that the IWG UK's superpower was connections and that "we have to create a network of networks with distributed power because enabling it to flourish without loss of momentum as the IWG Secretariat moves to new countries".

O'Keefe explained that the IWG UK had also identified three key themes, which are significant globally but particularly important in the UK and to the IWG funders: investment, leadership, visibility and portrayal. The UK Department for Business and Trade, in association with Deloitte and supported by the IWG, developed the Women's Sport Investment Accelerator programme, which is designed to boost investment and increase broadcast audiences for women's sport through mentoring, networking events and sessions on market insights, connecting women's sports rightsholders with industry experts and sports investors (Department for Business and Trade, 2023). This, O'Keefe described as a good example of the convening power of IWG, having "shone a light on the issue . . . got to some of the right players . . . and inspired collaboration". In addition, the IWG UK launched the Anita White Fund, to support women sport leaders around the world (https://iwgwomenandsport.org/programmes/anita-white-fund/), and is partnering with UNESCO on their Fit For Life programme (www.unesco.org/en/fit4life).

Progress since End Date

This book is published at the end of the first full year of the IWG UK Secretariat. O'Keefe felt that at this early stage "the conversation about the inequalities and what needs to happen is more visible, there are clearly networks and connections, and there is a growing momentum". Interestingly, Phelps indicated that the process of bidding to host the IWG "itself brought people together and encouraged them to work together, and have some really difficult conversations", and so even just preparing the bid had positive outcomes domestically.

While it is too early to state what outcomes and progress have been achieved by the IWG UK Secretariat, O'Keefe explained that "we have a really clear and well received strategy focusing IWG on where we can add most value". She saw the IWG Insight Hub, inherited from the IWG NZ, as key to providing "an accessible front door" into knowledge, insights, and research from around the globe, particularly if this is made available to the people who could advocate and deliver change for gender equality.

Looking Forward

For both Phelps and O'Keefe, a key issue is the fact that the investment in women's sport is still not equal to men's, and it is only recently that people are starting to strategically attend to the issues and resources required to maximise performance for women in sport. Phelps recognised that this is not the case in all regions of the world, and there remains gender inequality in many countries and cultures. Phelps also reflected on the IWG itself, which she feels is

> still very dominated by quite academic research and rarely . . . translates that into a practical outcome. So, actually we need to focus, we do need the research because it's incredibly important, but we need to make sure that there are practitioners also looking at how do we now use this and giving that equal weight in terms of making it happen.

She expressed concern that, where there is commercial success in women's sport, people may feel that the problem has been solved, and so the evidence needs to be informing practice.

This also informed the views of Phelps and O'Keefe on the Brighton Declaration, which they felt retains relevance but that there is a need to follow up with signatories to reignite their work with the IWG to advocate and demonstrate the case for change. This was highlighted in a report produced by the IWG UK, which identified that only 3.7% of signatories of the Brighton Declaration made reference to their connection with the IWG on their website (Pike & Richards, 2023). Phelps believed that the IWG needs to align itself better with global consortiums working in the women and sport space and to work more collaboratively and strategically to identify the overlaps and gaps in order to address them. Phelps and O'Keefe also shared views expressed by others that the benefits of moving the Secretariat every four years to impact on the host country and local needs are counter-balanced by the fact that it takes a year to secure funding and personnel to establish the new Secretariat, by which time some of the momentum of the previous Secretariat and World

Conference is lost. O'Keefe questioned, "how do you maintain the momentum, how do you make sure that lessons are learned from previous years", while Phelps wondered whether "the answer would be to have a permanent Secretariat", a proposal that had been recommended by an IWG Ad Hoc Committee in 2010 (Oglesby, 2010).

When asked what one change would have the biggest impact for women in sport, Phelps responded that

> if we want to change behaviours and change culture, we need legislation that will do that . . . the one thing that I would love to see . . . would be a way to ensure that kids grow up . . . where they have to share the sports facilities, where they can see and understand the contribution that both boys and girls at a young age can make to sport and to the team. I think that would not just change the women in sport movement, but I think it would change society in every aspect.

The main focus for Phelps and O'Keefe going forward is to challenge systemic bias. O'Keefe outlined a need for "rewiring the sports system, which was never designed for women and girls". In order to move from "fixing the women" to "fixing the system", Phelps explained the need for resource and investment: "I'm increasingly thinking that actually, it's just about sheer numbers and just reaching that tipping point. If you've got enough women together in a mixed sports organisation eventually they'll win the day because they'll have more votes". In so doing, she recognised that those currently holding positions of power fear "change" because there will inevitably be some loss in order to accommodate more women in senior roles. The future challenge and opportunities for the IWG are summed up in the words of Phelps outlining how to address this fear of change:

> I think we probably need to talk about that, and about how that is compensated for by having a better environment and a better society for everyone, and a better sports movement for everyone, and a more robust and resilient sector, both commercially, health wise, societally.

References

Department for Business and Trade. (2023, October 31). *New women's sport investment scheme kicks off first round with seven sports represented.* www.gov.uk/government/news/new-womens-sport-investment-scheme-kicks-off-first-round-with-seven-sports-represented. 31 2023

Matthews, J. J. K. (2020). The Brighton conference on women and sport. *Sport in History, 41*(1), 98–130. https//doi.org/10.1080/17460263.2020.1730943

Oglesby, C. (2010, March 15). *Report of the ad hoc committee on new IWG structure.* Anita White Collection: University of Chichester.

Pike, E., & Richards, S. (2023). *A look into the Brighton declaration signatories* [Unpublished report]. University of Hertfordshire.

10 Conclusion

Writing a history of the International Working Group on Women and Sport (IWG) to commemorate 30 years since its establishment became much more than the story of a network. The decision to form an IWG took place in a period of social and political turmoil, and the issues faced in the subsequent three decades reflect global socio-political progress as well as emergent new problems for women, sport, and human rights. The principles on which the IWG was established have brought enormous progress and benefits, as well as their own challenges. For example, the decision to create an unconstituted network rather than a formal organisation demonstrates what is possible when bringing together individual and organisational change-agents unrestricted by formal processes, but also what tensions and challenges informal governance can bring. Similarly, the decision to advocate for action and change has had a positive impact on global and local practice, with some host countries citing legislative change as a result of their term as the IWG Secretariat. However, this also leaves questions about accountability and how not to leave behind those communities where calls for radical change may conflict with social and cultural ideology (see Pike & Matthews, 2014).

This book is structured around each consecutive Secretariat, and the way that these are established and the personnel involved is informative of how networks work. Those interviewed for this book often drew on their own experiences of gender inequality in their sporting or professional backgrounds to inform how they operated in their IWG roles. The ways in which members were selected varied across different Secretariats largely due to the lack of a formal Constitution or Terms of Reference. One co-Chair has been appointed by the host country and the other either appointed by the Global Executive or through advertisement. IWG Board Members were generally appointed by their regional organisations or co-opted based on expertise. During the terms of some Secretariats, there have been calls for an Extended Board, and the Australia Secretariat proposed that governments who had supported previous Secretariats should have a special status as IWG members, but these proposals have not been consistently retained. Several interviewees expressed the value of male allies while also indicating that those in positions of power (who were

72 Conclusion

usually men) felt threatened by the empowerment of women and the potential loss of their own influence. A further challenge is that the IWG operates in the English language, and Secretariats have to adopt strategies to facilitate communication and collaboration, as outlined by some of the former hosts interviewed for this book.

The IWG was deliberately established as a network, rather than a membership organisation, in order to be different to traditional, male-dominated, models of sports governance. This created incredible opportunities to be inclusive of numerous stakeholders from governmental and non-governmental agencies, sports councils, higher education, national and international sports organisations. Each quadrennial, the Secretariat relocates to a new host country, bringing opportunities to use the IWG to leverage action, visibility, and policy change in different regions of the world, in some cases bringing about change through sport that impacted on wider society. However, each Secretariat also identified the challenges of this, with some indicating that the women and sport movement lost momentum every four years as the new Secretariat learned its role and established a new team. In addition, in order to fund the IWG Secretariat, there were often multiple host organisations, each of which placed demands on the Secretariat. The Secretariats demonstrated impressive creativity and flexibility in securing funds from different organisations. However, it also meant that members of the Secretariat found themselves reporting to multiple stakeholders, including their funders, government agencies, as well as the IWG Global Executive, sometimes with conflicting priorities and perspectives.

In addition to domestic challenges, what also became clear during the interviews was the tensions between different international groups. For example, while the International Olympic Committee (IOC) has actively supported the IWG World Conference and signed the Brighton Declaration, in the early stages of developing the IWG the IOC declined an invitation to have a seat as a member and, instead, established its own Women and Sport Committee. The relationship between the IWG, WomenSport International (WSI), and the International Association of Physical Education and Sport for Girls and Women (IAPESGW) have a long history of tension, with each new Secretariat negotiating respectful ways of collaborating. The most recent Secretariat is now also working alongside the Global Observatory for Gender Equality and Sport, which, in turn, has raised questions as to whether the name of the IWG should be changed from the International Working Group on Women and Sport, to the IWG for Gender Equality and Sport. In 2010, an Ad Hoc Committee on a new IWG Structure was formed, to review the mission, aims, values and operating principles of the IWG "to enhance democratic practices and transparency within the IWG Core Group and international Network" (Oglesby, 2010). Proposals included whether the IWG should become a member organisation (noting this may impact on other member organisations such as WSI and IAPESGW), or to restructure into two segments, one which

Conclusion 73

focuses on the World Conference and shifts to a new site each quadrennial, the other being a permanent Secretariat to coordinate and monitor the rest of the work of the IWG. These discussions continue to the present day.

When the Brighton Declaration was formulated in 1994, and updated in 2014, it was the only global set of principles for gender equality and sport. In 2020, UN Women and the IOC launched the Sport for Generation Equality Framework, and the IOC also has its own Gender Equality and Inclusion Framework. These raise questions about how the IWG, UN Women and the IOC might best collaborate to support individuals and organisations who may be confused by these multiple sets of frameworks and declarations. This is particularly pertinent given "the concern that many organisations have not translated their endorsement of the Brighton Declaration and stated commitment into the sort of actions or change that really makes a difference" (IWG, 1998), and so further attention needs to be directed to how to support and monitor change that relates to these frameworks and their stated principles.

The advocacy work, and reports on progress, of the IWG and other international women and sport groups includes ongoing debates around participation and equal rights, as well as the relatively recent discussion around complex issues regarding sexuality and sexual harassment, intersectionality (particularly related to racism, issues in the Global South, socio-economic issues), and gender identities including trans and intersex issues. The information presented in this book demonstrates that, while there remain tensions between some groups, there is evidence of more coordinated activities through the IWG network, such as the IOC with sport, United Nations Children's Fund (UNICEF) with charities, and the UN and many governmental groups with politics. The commitment to collaboration has been a strategic priority, and a key strength, of the IWG since its inception.

In sharing the voices of those involved with the first eight IWG Secretariats and World Conferences on Women and Sport, a number of recurrent themes and recommendations have emerged from their experiences.

- The IWG is a network rather than an organisation, and is answerable to multiple agencies including funders, host organisations, and the Global Executive. Future Secretariats may wish to learn from best practice of previous hosts, and reflect on how they might best navigate this for greatest effect.
- In relocating the IWG Secretariat each quadrennial, there are tremendous benefits in leveraging visibility and change in different regions, but also a potential loss of momentum. A consideration for the IWG going forward is whether to establish a permanent Secretariat while retaining the benefits of moving the World Conference to a different country/region every four years to retain the global reach of the IWG.
- The IWG Secretariat has been hosted on most continents, and held meetings across the globe. There remain challenges for women and sport in

many societies and cultures, often located in regions which have not hosted the Secretariat, and future IWG Secretariats may wish to consider how they continue to collaborate with, and support, women and sport in these communities.
- Since the establishment of the IWG, further international organisations, networks, and frameworks for gender equality have been created. This demonstrates greater understanding of the need to support women and sport, but there remain some tensions and confusion for future IWG Secretariats to navigate.
- In reviewing the saliency of the Brighton Plus Helsinki 2014 Declaration in the light of newer Declarations and Frameworks, each former IWG Secretariat reinforced the need to ensure that signing these Declarations leads to action and positive change for gender equality in sport.

The IWG was formed at the first World Conference on Women and Sport in 1994. In 2024, it celebrates its 30th anniversary, having demonstrably influenced policy and practice around the globe as outlined in the chapters of this book. In the closing ceremony of the 1994 conference, the Acting Director General of the GB Sports Council said:

> Let us hope that in ten or twenty years' time at the third, fourth or fifth conferences of this type after Brighton, that delegates (perhaps even some of us) will look back and identify that this was the conference that agreed that collective and global change was necessary and it was here that the process began.
>
> (Casey, 1994, p. 129)

As we look back, not in ten or twenty years, but thirty years from this statement, approaching the ninth IWG World Conference, it is possible to see the remarkable development of the IWG global network. As the Secretariat and Conference has moved from country to country, continent to continent, with increasing numbers of signatories to the Brighton Declaration and delegates at the World Conferences, there is demonstrable visibility for, and acknowledgement of, gender equality issues in sport among government and major sport bodies, with subsequent legislative change in a number of countries.

None of this was achieved easily. The achievements are testament to those who organised and attended the 1994 conference, those individual women leaders who have been prepared to persevere in the face of opposition and adversity, and those who have led the IWG through subsequent Secretariats. Their commitment to collective and global change over the following three decades has made sport a better place for women, and many societies a better place for women's involvement in sport.

Reference List

Casey, D. (1994). Developing international strategies. In *An international conference – Women, sport and the challenge of change – Conference Proceedings* (pp. 125–129). GB Sports Council.

International Working Group on Women and Sport. (1998). *Women and sport: From Brighton to Windhoek, facing the challenge.* UK Sports Council.

Oglesby, C. (2010, March 15). *Report of the ad hoc committee on new IWG structure.* Anita White Collection: University of Chichester.

Pike, E. C. J., & Matthews, J. J. K. (2014). A post-colonial critique of the international 'movements' for women and sexuality in sport. In J. Hargreaves & E. Anderson (Eds.) *Routledge handbook of sport, gender, and sexuality.* Routledge.

Appendices

Appendix 1
IWG Members/Global Executive

1994–1998		
Katia Mascagni	NGO Representative: IOC	Switzerland
Elizabeth Darlison	NGO Representative: WSI	Australia
Clemencia Anaya Maya	Regional Representative: Americas	Colombia
Mien Gondowidjojo	Regional Representative: Asia	Indonesia
Kereyn Smith	Regional Representative: Oceania	New Zealand
Debbie Simms	Regional Representative: Oceania	Australia
Sue Neill	Host of next World Conference	Canada
Judy Kent	Host of next World Conference	Canada
1998–2002		
Nawal El Moukawatel	NGO Representative: IOC and CONFEJES	Morocco
Lu Shengring	NGO Representative: International Badminton Federation	China
Carole Oglesby	NGO Representative: WSI	USA
Chris Shelton	NGO Representative: WSI	USA
Nabilah Ahmed Abdulrahman	NGO Representative: IAPESGW	Egypt
Margaret Talbot	NGO Representative: IAPESGW	United Kingdom
Clemencia Anaya Maya	Regional Representative: Americas	Colombia
Anra Bobb	Regional Representative: Caribbean	Trinidad and Tobago
Birgitta Kervinen	Regional Representative: Europe	Finland
Alisi Tabete	Regional Representative: Oceania	Fiji
Judy Kent	Co-opted (Commonwealth Games Federation)	Canada
Debora Cubagee	Co-opted	Ghana
Etsuko Ogasawara	Co-opted	Japan
Pirjo Puskala	Co-opted	Finland
Carole Garoes	Co-opted	Namibia

(*Continued*)

Appendix 1

(Continued)

1998–2002

Name	Role	Country
Kari Fasting	NGO Representative: WSI	Norway
Margaret Talbot	NGO Representative: IAPESGW	United Kingdom
Chris Shelton	Regional Representative: Americas	USA
Hon. Pendukini Iivula-Ithana	Regional Representative: Africa	Namibia
Annabel Pennefather	Regional Representative: Asia	Singapore
Chantal Amade-Escot	Regional Representative: Europe	France
Lois Fordham	Regional Representative: Oceania	Australia
Anita White	Co-opted expert	United Kingdom
Beatrice Hess	Co-opted	France
Lilamani de Soysa	Co-opted	Sri Lanka

2006–2010

Name	Role	Country
Kari Fasting	NGO Representative: WSI	Norway
Darlene Kluka	NGO Representative: IAPESGW (2006–2009)	USA
Tansin Benn	NGO Representative: IAPESGW (2009–2010)	United Kingdom
Chris Shelton	Regional Representative: Americas (2006–2008) Co-opted (2008–2010)	USA
Clemencia Anaya Maya	Regional Representative: Americas (2008–2010)	Colombia
Hon. Pendukini Iivula-Ithana	Regional Representative: Africa	Namibia
Aneesa Al-Hitma	Regional Representative: Asia (2006–2008)	Qatar
YB Dato' Seri Azalina Dato' Othman Said	Regional Representative: Asia (2008–2010)	Malaysia
Amanda Athina Kyriakidou	Regional Representative: Europe (2006–2008)	Cyprus
Amanda Bennett	Regional Representative: Europe (2009–2010)	United Kingdom
Susie Yee	Regional Representative: Oceania	Fiji
Lilamani de Soysa	Co-opted	Switzerland
Lydia la Riviere	Co-opted	Netherlands
Etsuko Ogasawara	Co-opted	Japan
Flora Eteta'a	Co-opted	Cameroon

2010–2014

Name	Role	Country
Kari Fasting	NGO Representative: WSI	Norway
Tansin Benn	NGO Representative: IAPESGW (2010–2013)	United Kingdom
Rosa Lopez de D'Amico	NGO Representative: IAPESGW (2013–2014)	Venezuela

Appendix 1   81

Clemencia Anaya Maya	Regional Representative: Americas	Colombia
Natalya Sipovich	Regional Representative: Asia	Kazakhstan
Evelina Georgiades	Regional Representative: Europe	Cyprus
Kristiina Pekkola	Regional Representative: Europe	Sweden
Kristina Thuree	Regional Representative: Europe (2013–2014)	Sweden
Matilda Mwaba	Regional Representative: Africa	Zambia
Susie Yee	Regional Representative: Oceania	Fiji
Valiollah Saint-Louis Gilmus	Co-opted (CONFEJES)	Haiti
Malini Rajasegaran	Co-opted (Women and Disability)	Malaysia
2014–2018		
Kari Fasting	NGO Representative: WSI	Norway
Rosa Lopez de D'Amico	NGO Representative: IAPESGW (2013–2014)	Venezuela
Matilda Mwaba	Regional Representative: Africa	Zambia
Valiollah Saint-Louis Gilmus	Co-opted (CONFEJES)	Haiti
Etsuko Ogasawara	Regional Representative: Asia	Japan
Karen Morrison	Regional Representative: Americas	USA
Kristina Thuree	Regional Representative: Europe	Sweden
Susie Yee	Regional Representative: Oceania	Fiji
Lilamani de Soysa	Co-opted	Japan
2018–2022		
Rosa Diketmuller	NGO Representative: IAPESGW	Austria
Diane Huffman	NGO Representative: WSI	Canada
Game Mothibi	Regional Representative: Africa	Botswana
Karen Morrison	Regional Representative: Americas	USA
Etsuko Ogasawara	Regional Representative: Asia	Japan
Sallie Barker	Regional Representative: Europe	UK
Emma Waiwai	Regional Representative: Oceania	Papua New Guinea
Lilamani de Soysa	Co-opted	Switzerland
Fiona Allan	Co-opted	New Zealand
Louisette-Renée Thobi Etame Ndedl	Co-opted	Mali

(*Continued*)

Appendix 1

(Continued)

2022–2026

Rosa Diketmuller	NGO Representative: IAPESGW	Austria
Diane Huffman	NGO Representative: WSI	Canada
Game Mothibi	Regional Representative: Africa	Botswana
Rosaura Mendez Gamboa	Regional Representative: Americas	Costa Rica
Etsuko Ogasawara	Regional Representative: Asia	Japan
Sallie Barker	Regional Representative: Europe	UK
Carolyn Ngiraidis	Regional Representative: Oceania	Republic of Palau
Lilamani de Soysa	Co-opted	Switzerland
Fiona Allan	Co-opted	New Zealand
Louisette-Renée Thobi Etame NdedI	Co-opted	Cameroon

Appendix 2
IWG Annual Meetings

Year	IWG Secretariat	Venue
1994		Brighton, United Kingdom (First World Conference)
		Ottawa, Canada (AGM)
1995	United Kingdom/Namibia	Jakarta, Indonesia (AGM)
1996	United Kingdom/Namibia	Gold Coast, Australia (AGM)
1997	United Kingdom/Namibia	Auckland, New Zealand (AGM)
1998	United Kingdom/Namibia/Canada	Windhoek, Namibia (Second World Conference)
		Bogota, Colombia (Additional Meeting)
1999	Canada	Alexandria, Egypt (AGM)
2000	Canada	Helsinki, Finland (AGM)
2001	Canada	Kumamoto, Japan (AGM)
2002	Canada/Japan	Montreal, Canada (Third World Conference)
		Paris, France (Additional Meeting)
2003	Japan	Bisham Abbey, United Kingdom (AGM)
2004	Japan	Smith College, United States of America (AGM)
		Marrakech, Morocco (Additional Meeting)
		London, United Kingdom; Berlin, Germany; Kumamoto, Japan (conference planning meetings)
2005	Japan	Singapore, Malaysia (AGM)
2006	Japan/Australia	Kumamoto, Japan (Fourth World Conference)
2007	Australia	Kuala Lumpur (Special Meeting)
2008	Australia	Mikkeli, Finland (AGM)
2009	Australia	Bogota, Colombia (AGM)
2010	Australia/Finland	Sydney, Australia (Fifth World Conference)
2011	Finland	Paris, France (AGM)
2012	Finland	Tokyo, Japan (AGM)
2013	Finland	Doha, Qatar (AGM)
2014	Finland/Botswana	Helsinki (Sixth World Conference)
2015	Botswana	San Diego, California, USA (AGM)
2016	Botswana	Stockholm, Sweden (AGM)
2017	Botswana	Tokyo, Japan (AGM)
2018	Botswana/New Zealand	Gaborone, Botswana (Seventh World Conference)

(*Continued*)

(Continued)

Year	IWG Secretariat	Venue
2019	New Zealand	London, United Kingdom (AGM)
2020	New Zealand	Virtual (AGM)
2021	New Zealand	Virtual (AGM)
2022	New Zealand/ United Kingdom	Auckland, New Zealand (Eighth World Conference)
2023	United Kingdom	Costa Rica (AGM)
2024	United Kingdom	

Index

Note: Page numbers in **bold** indicate a table on the corresponding page.

Adriaanse, Johanna **4**, 32–39, 40
African Women in Sport Association 14
Anita White Collection 3, 41
Anita White Foundation 3, 41, 43
Anita White Fund 68
Asia Women in Sports 52
Auckland **6**, 57, **83**, **84**
Australia Sports Commission 33

Birmingham 68
Botswana Big 5 51
Botswana Sports Commission 50
Brighton Conference 3, 7, 8–10, 11, 12, 19, 40, 41, 42, 43, 44, 48, 66
Brighton Declaration 1, 9, 10, 11, 13, 14, 15, 19, 23, 29, 30, 40, 42, 43, 44, 53, 61, 62, 69, 72, 73, 74
Brighton Plus Helsinki 2014 Declaration 15, 40, 44, 46, 62, 74

Cameron, Trice **4**, 18
Canadian Association for the Advancement of Women and Sport and Physical Activity (CAAWS) 19, 20
Champions of Change Coalition 39
Commonwealth Games Federation (CGF) 14, 61, **79**
CONFEJES (Conférence des ministres de la jeunesse et des sports de la Francophonie) 20, 32, **79**, **81**
Covid-19 1, 38, 45, 56, 60, 62, 64, 68

European Non-Governmental Sports Organisation (ENGSO) 35, 41
European Sport Conference Working Group on Women and Sport (ESCWGWS) 8

Froggatt, Rachel **5**, 56–63

Gaborone **6**, 16, **83**
Garoes, Carol 12
Gender Equality and Inclusion Framework 73
Global North 11, 38
Global Observatory for Gender Equality and Sport 2, 15, 21, 49, 52, 72; *see also* International Observatory
Global South 53, 73
Great Britain Sports Council 1

Hansen, Andy **4**, 13
Heinilä, Terhi **4**, 40–45
Helsinki **6**, 39, 43, **83**

Iivula-Ithana, Pendukeni **4**, 10, 11, 12, 13, 19, **80**
Indigenous Statement on Call to Action 61

International Association of Physical Education and Sport for Girls and Women (IAPESGW) 2, 11, 33, 37, 42, 43, 48, 49, 62, 63, 72, 79, 80, **81, 82**
International Federations 13, 15, 38, 42, 43, 61, 67
International Observatory 21, 33, 36, 37; *see also* Global Observatory for Gender Equality and Sport
International Olympic Committee (IOC) 10, 13, 14, 21, 26, 27, 34, 42, 43, 59, 61, 66, 67, 72, 73, **79**
International Paralympic Committee (IPC) 14, 32, 61
International Strategy 9
IWG Global Executive 3, 31, 34, 35, 49, 50, 54, 61, 67, 71, 72, 73, **79–82**
IWG Insight Hub 31, 53, 60, 62,69
IWG Progress Report 13, 14, 22, 28, 31, 37, 43, 48, 51, 53, 62

Japanese Association for Women Sports (JWS) 25
Japanese Basic Strategic Plan 29
Japanese Gender Equality Law 27

Kervinen, Birgitta **4**, 35, 41, **79**
Kuala Lumpur 35, 36, **83**
Kumamoto **6**, 24, 26, 32, 35, **83**
Kumamoto Commitment to Collaboration 30, 31, 36

Lovett, Raewyn **5**, 56, 64, 66

Maphorisa, Ruth **5**, 46, 48, 51, 56
Mattila, Raija **4**, 40–45, 46, 48
MINEPS (International Conference of Ministers and Senior Officials Responsible for Physical Education and Sport) 21
Montreal **6**, 18, 20, 21, 33, **84**
Montreal Tool Kit 22
Mothibi, Game **5**, 46–55, **81, 82**

National Coaching Foundation 65
Neill, Sue **4**, 18–23, 24–31, 32, **79**

Ogasawara, Etsuko **4**, 24–31, 35, **79, 80, 81, 82**
Oglesby, Carole **4, 5**, 35, 46–55, 70, 72, **79**
O'Keefe, Lisa **5**, 64–70

Phelps, Annemarie **5**, 64–70
Pike, Elizabeth 3, **5**, 68

Scoretz, Deena **4**, 18
Sport and Recreation Alliance (formerly Central Council of Physical Recreation) 66, 67, 68
Sport England 65, 66, 67
Sport for Generation Equality 62, 73
Sydney **6**, 34, 38, **83**
Sydney Scoreboard 38, 60

TAFISA (The Association For International Sport for All) 49, 52

UK Sport 66, 67
UNESCO (United Nations Educational, Scientific and Cultural Organization) 21, 32, 41, 67
UNICEF (United Nations Children's Fund) 73
United Nations (UN) 10, 32, 36, 37, 39, 49, 52, 62
United Nations Beijing Declaration and Platform for Action (1995) 2
United Nations Division for the Advancement of Women (UNDAW) 37
United Nations Sustainable Development Goals 44
University of Hertfordshire 67
UN Women 38, 73

White, Anita 2, 3, **4**, 7–17, 26, 28, 36, 42, 47, 48, **80**
Windhoek **6**, 12, 14, 18, 19, **83**

Windhoek Call to Action 14, 22
Women in Sport (formerly Women's
 Sports Foundation) 65
Women in Sport Aotearoa 57
Women in Sport Botswana 47, 50

WomenSport International (WSI)
 formerly Women's International
 Sports Coalition 2, 10, 11, 14, 32,
 33, 37, 38, 42, 43, 48, 49, 62, 63,
 72, **79**, **80**, **81**, **82**

Taylor & Francis eBooks

www.taylorfrancis.com

A single destination for eBooks from Taylor & Francis with increased functionality and an improved user experience to meet the needs of our customers.

90,000+ eBooks of award-winning academic content in Humanities, Social Science, Science, Technology, Engineering, and Medical written by a global network of editors and authors.

TAYLOR & FRANCIS EBOOKS OFFERS:

- A streamlined experience for our library customers
- A single point of discovery for all of our eBook content
- Improved search and discovery of content at both book and chapter level

REQUEST A FREE TRIAL
support@taylorfrancis.com

For Product Safety Concerns and Information please contact our EU representative GPSR@taylorandfrancis.com
Taylor & Francis Verlag GmbH, Kaufingerstraße 24, 80331 München, Germany

www.ingramcontent.com/pod-product-compliance
Lightning Source LLC
Chambersburg PA
CBHW071823230426
43670CB00013B/2551